The Uncanonical Jewish Books

The
Uncanonical Jewish Books

A SHORT INTRODUCTION TO THE
APOCRYPHA AND OTHER JEWISH
WRITINGS, 200 B C.—100 A D.

BY

WILLIAM JOHN FERRAR, M.A.
LATE SCHOLAR OF HERTFORD COLLEGE, OXFORD

WIPF & STOCK · Eugene, Oregon

Wipf and Stock Publishers
199 W 8th Ave, Suite 3
Eugene, OR 97401

The Uncannonical Jewish Books
A Short Introduction to the Apocrypha
and Other Jewish Writings, 200 B.C. - 100 A.D.
By Ferrar, William John
Softcover ISBN-13: 978-1-6667-3479-9
Hardcover ISBN-13: 978-1-6667-9105-1
eBook ISBN-13: 978-1-6667-9106-8
Publication date 9/7/2021
Previously published by SPCK, 1918

This edition is a scanned facsimile of
the original edition published in 1918.

PREFACE

THE object of this Introduction is to provide a short account not only of the books in the Church Apocrypha, but of the other Jewish writings from 200 B.C. to A.D. 100, which should be now occupying the attention of those interested in the New Testament. For without some knowledge of the contemporary literature of the period, we lose the chief key to the understanding of the world to which Christ came, and the atmosphere in which the Church was born

It is obvious that in so short a compass as this volume allows, it is only possible to give an impression of each book, and that statements have constantly to be made dogmatically which would need considerable discussion in a larger work. The writer has done his best to present the sanest views of the best scholars, and can claim that nothing has been put down that has not the support of competent scholars of the present time. And he hopes that this " conspectus " or " bird's-eye view " of a great field of knowledge and research will give a trustworthy impression of the general trend of literary activity during the period. Such an impression cannot fail to be of use in the appreciation of the New Testament; and therefore, wherever necessary, attention has been drawn to any instances of a direct connection between these writers and those of the canonical books or to any actual quotation. He chiefly hopes that readers will be led to read the uncanonical writers for themselves, and the great modern books on the period, and making their

own comparisons and conclusions, may thus secure
new and abiding light on the Gospel and the Church.

He has to acknowledge with deep thankfulness
the help afforded by Dr. Charles's great edition of
those books, *The Apocrypha and Pseudepigrapha of
the Old Testament*, the articles in Hastings's *Dictionary of the Bible* and the *Encyclopædia Biblica,* and
Dr. W. O E. Oesterley's *The Books of the Apocrypha,*
without which this Introduction would have been
impossible.

East Finchley,
March, 1918.

CONTENTS

APOCRYPHA

TABLE OF PERIODS OF THE WRITING OF THE UNCANONICAL BOOKS

	B C				A D.		
	200–150	150–100	100–50	50–1	1–50	50–100	After 100
	Tobit	Prayer of Azariah	I Maccabees	Judith	I Esdras	I Baruch	III Baruch
	Ecclesiasticus	Bel and the Dragon	II Maccabees	Wisdom of Solomon	Assumption of Moses	Adam and Eve	Sibylline Oracles, v.
	I. Enoch (1)	Jubilees	III Maccabees		II Enoch	Martyrdom of Isaiah	II Esdras (final writing)
	I Enoch (4)	I. Enoch (3)	Prayer of Manasseh		IV Maccabees	Sibylline Oracles, iv.	
		Testament of XII Patriarchs	Susanna			II. Baruch	
		Sibylline Oracles, iii.	Additions to Esther			Constituents of II Esdras	
			I Enoch (2)				
			I Enoch (5)				
			Psalms of Solomon				

BIBLIOGRAPHY OF WORKS IN ENGLISH

Schurer   A HISTORY OF THE JEWISH PEOPLE IN THE TIME
   OF JESUS CHRIST   English translation, 1890–1   Ger-
   man ed 3rd and 4th, 1901–9
Edwyn Bevan   Jerusalem under the High Priests   1904.
   The House of Seleucus   1902.
Toy   Christianity and Judaism   1891.
Oesterley   Wisdom of Jesus, Son of Sirach   1912
   Ecclesiasticus   (Cambridge Bible)   1912
   The Doctrine of the Last Things   1908
   The Books of the Apocrypha   1914
   The Evolution of the Messianic Idea   1908
Oesterley and Box   The Religion and Worship of the Syna-
   gogue   1911
Burkitt.   JEWISH AND CHRISTIAN APOCALYPSES   1914
Charles.   Eschatology, Hebrew, Jewish and Christian   1913.
S. Davidson   The Canon of the Bible   1877.
Ryle.   The Canon of the Old Testament   1892
Robertson Smith   The Old Testament in the Jewish Church.
   1895.
Swete   The Old Testament in Greek   1899
Charles   THE APOCRYPHA AND PSEUDEPIGRAPHA OF THE OLD
   TESTAMENT   (Edited with many scholars)   1913
   Book of Enoch   1912
   Testaments of the Twelve Patriarchs   1908
   Assumption of Moses.   1897.
   Ascension of Isaiah.   1900
   Secrets of Enoch   (With Morfill)   1896.
   Apocalypse of Baruch.   1896.
Ryle and James.   The Psalms of Solomon.   1891
Rendel Harris.   The Odes and Psalms of Solomon   1911.
Driver.   Introduction to Old Testament.   1891.
Gregg.   Wisdom of Solomon.   1909.
Hart.   Ecclesiasticus   1909
Bissell.   1st Book of Maccabees   (Lange-Schaff)   1880.
Fairweather and Black.   1st Book of Maccabees.   (Cambridge
   Bible)   1897.

Goodrich Book of Wisdom. 1913.
Bensly and James Fourth Book of Ezra (Latin Version) 1895
Box. The Ezra-Apocalypse 1912
Hastings. Dictionary of the Bible
Encycl of Religion and Ethics
Encyclopædia Biblica
Jewish Encyclopædia.
} General and Special Articles
Editions of Apocryphal Books in Lange-Schaff's Commentary Wace's Apocrypha Modern Reader's Bible, Temple Bible, and the Variorum Apocrypha.
S P C K Texts I —Aramaic Papyri Cowley.
Wisdom of Ben-Sira Oesterley.
Book of Enoch Charles.
Book of Jubilees Charles
Testaments of Twelve Patriarchs Charles.
Ascension of Isaiah Charles
Apocalypse of Ezra (2 Esdras) Box.
Apocalypse of Baruch Charles
Assumption of Moses Ferrar
Biblical Antiquities of Philo James.
II —Wisdom of Solomon. Oesterley.
Sibylline Oracles Bate.
Letter of Aristeas Thackeray
Selections from Josephus Thackeray.
3 and 4 Maccabees Emmet.

(Large type indicates general indispensability for study.)

THE

UNCANONICAL JEWISH BOOKS

I. ESDRAS (THE GREEK EZRA)

THIS book presents many critical problems, which
it is impossible in so small a space to do more than
mention. It is the book which appears in our official
Apocrypha as 1 Esdras, the contents of which run
parallel to those in the books of Ezra and Nehemiah,
and which by its divergencies from the latter raises
important questions.

It was written in Greek at any time during the
first century A.D. by one of the Pharisaic school,
most probably *not* in Palestine, with the object of
glorifying everything connected with the Temple and
its worship, and exalting the fame and work of Ezra
the scribe. The rebuilding of the Temple represented to the Jewish mind the continuance of Israel's
sacrificial approach to God, and Ezra stood for the
importance of the Law The Altar and the Law
were the two great privileges of Israel. It is these
with which the writer is chiefly concerned, and he
seems to regard historical events as an unimportant
background to these two ideas.

1 Esdras seems to stand in the following relation
to the Biblical Ezra. The latter with Nehemiah was
originally the conclusion of the Chronicles, and an
integral part of them, written after the Exile in order
to give a special trend to Jewish historical ideas.
Chronicles was not at once admitted into the Canon,
as the ground was already covered by 1 and 2 Kings.
But as there was no record in the Hebrew Bible of

the events recorded in Ezra and Nehemiah, they
were recognized as canonical. And thus they appear
in the Septuagint as Esdras 1 and 2. But it is
significant that they are there placed *after* the book
we are considering, and also that Josephus uses our
book as his authority, and does not seem to recognize
the canonical account. The ground covered by the
two versions is not quite the same, for our book
embraces 2 Chron. xxxv.–xxxvi 1–23, in addition to
Ezra and Nehemiah vii. 6–viii. 12, while the interesting passage iii. 1–v. 3 has nothing corresponding to
it in the Biblical material.

The contents of 1 Esdras are as follow—

i. 1–24, Josiah's Passover, 25–33, death at Megiddo;
34–58, reigns of kings to Fall of Jerusalem
(586 B.C.).

ii 1–15, Cyrus's decree to rebuild Jerusalem
(538 B.C); 16–30, Samaritans' letter to Artaxerxes, and rebuilding ceases till Darius (520 B C).

iii. 1–iv. 46, Zerubbabel's victory in the competi-
tion; iv. 47–v. 3, allowed to return and rebuild
walls and Temple.

v. 4–46, List of exiles; 46–65, rebuilding; 66–73,
the Samaritans cause suspension

vi. 1–6, Building of Temple begun; 7–34, letter
of Sisinnes and favourable reply of Darius.

vii. 1–15, Dedication and Passover (516 B C.).

viii. 1–ix. 36, Ezra comes by permission of Artaxerxes (458 B C); he brings Priests and Levites,
and stops mixed marriages.

ix. 37–55, He reads the Law of Moses (444 B.C.).

It will be seen by the above that our book differs
from the canonical—

(1) By reversing the order of the Persian kings,
which was in reality—

Cyrus (533–529 B.C),
Darius I. (522–486 B C),
Artaxerxes I. (465–425 B.C.),

although it starts correctly with Cyrus in ii. 1 *seq.*

(ii) By taking no account of Neh. i. 1–vii. 72, and thus making the story of Ezra continuous.

There is no doubt that the writer reflected a somewhat hazy view of the chronology of the Return from Exile in the Hebrew records which he strung together, and it is possible that portions of the Hebrew were already misplaced and names wrongly given. Dr. Oesterley supposes there were two Hebrew documents in existence, represented in translation respectively by the canonical Ezra and our book. The former is by no means historically impeccable, and the nearest approach to truth is probably to be found by combining the two accounts.

The story of the three young men and of Zerubbabel's victory, as has been said, is peculiar to the book It is a specimen of a type of Eastern tale familiar to readers of the *Arabian Nights*, and, of course, memorable for its great word : *Magna est veritas, et prævalet.* The young guardsmen in the story compete together to phrase the wisest sentence, and each puts his writing under Darius's pillow. The first writes, " Wine is the strongest ", the second, " The King is strongest " ; and Zerubbabel, " Women are strongest, but truth above all things beareth away the victory." Each sentence is next day defended at some length in the King's presence, Zerubbabel is proclaimed the winner, and craves as his reward the rebuilding of the Jewish walls and Temple. Dr. Oesterley suggests that this story, being such an obvious patch on the rest of the book, was an attempt made by a Hellenistic reviser to minimize what seemed to him an excessive stress on the personality of Ezra, and to present Zerubbabel, the more " prophetic " name, as also in the foreground of the picture.

Note —The fullest recent discussion of the problems connected with the book is contained in Prof C C. Torrey's *Ezra Studies* (Chicago University Press) ; 1909.

I. MACCABEES

THE First Book of Maccabees seems to have been written between 100 and 90 B.C., after the death of John Hyrcanus in 105 B.C. Our present Greek text bears many signs of having been translated from the Hebrew. The writer was "an ardent patriot and a rigid adherent of orthodox Judaism," and a native of Palestine. Dr. Oesterley ranks him with the Sadducees, and the writer's laudation of John Hyrcanus, who definitely broke with the Pharisaic party, would support this. Much that was good in Pharisaism, however, appealed strongly to him. He is a true historian with an easy flowing style, takes great pains to present original documents, and is in the main, in spite of an occasional tendency to exaggeration, unprejudiced and impartial. Of some of the later events recorded he was perhaps himself an eye-witness, and the graphic touches in the earlier history show him to have used the accounts of eye-witnesses.

The course covered by the story is from 175 B.C. to 135 B.C., *i. e.* from the accession of Antiochus Epiphanes to the death of Simon Maccabæus. Our limits of space make it impossible to follow in detail the course of the Maccabæan struggle. The story is readily accessible in the Apocrypha, and is told simply and straightforwardly, though it becomes involved in the somewhat tortuous history of the Seleucid dynasty. It groups itself round the commanding personalities of Mattathias, Judas — the "Maccabee," or "Hammerer," whose greatness conferred his name on his whole family—and of Jonathan and Simon. It records how by the firm stand made by one family, combined with fortunate external

14

events, the Jewish people, shorn of political independence, with their religious liberty jeopardized, brow-
beaten by a powerful monarch, and cankered with
inward decay, reasserted their national independence,
re-established their Altar and Priesthood, and became
amid the jarring politics of their neighbours, " the
deciding factor " of the stability of thrones. It shows
how by the faithfulness of a determined few the
capture of Judaism by the spirit of Hellenism was
prevented, and the policy of the clique who had
" joined themselves to the Gentiles, and sold themselves to do evil," effectually countered. The great
career of Judas, untimely in its end, assured religious
freedom ; the energy and diplomacy of Jonathan and
the establishment of the High Priesthood in his family
made the Maccabees—or as they came to be called,
the Hasmoneans—supreme in Church and State, all
power being centralized in their persons, while under
Simon and John the Jews won their way to an
independence which was only destroyed by Pompey
in 63 B C.

The official documents preserved in this book
naturally arouse inquiry. Can they be trusted as
authentic ? In the main, yes. " The documentary
sources shed a most valuable light on the external
policy of the Jews as well as on the important *rôle* they
played in shaping Syrian politics " [1] The ones that
rouse suspicion are the " Letter from Jonathan to the
Spartans " (xii 6–18), the letter of the Spartans to
Simon (xiv. 20–22), and the letter from Lucius, the
Roman Consul, to Ptolemy (xv. 16–21), though even
beneath these there may be a historical foundation.
There is no reason to doubt the genuineness of the
letter of the King of Sparta to Onias (xii. 20–23), the
treaty of alliance between Rome and the Jews (viii.
23–32), or the letters from Syrian kings to the Jewish
leaders.

The religious outlook of the writer differs from that
of the Old Testament. He refrains from emphasizing

[1] Oesterley, p 423

the intervention of God in the Jewish struggles, and
indeed does not once mention God by name. He
believes strongly, however, in Providence, and also
in the need of human energy. " This very sensible
religious attitude, which is as far removed from
scepticism as it is from fatalism, fully corresponds to
the writer's sober impartiality as a historian."

His gift of characterization has placed the great
figures of the Maccabees in the gallery of the world's
heroes. He has filled the spaces of an age, of which
without his help our knowledge would be scanty, with
magnificent figures, vivid and full of individuality.
He has given a trustworthy picture of much that went
to make Jewish society what it was at the time of
our Lord's birth, and preserved the memory of what
must have been considered by His contemporaries a
great heritage, but also a terrible reproach in their
final state of servitude—the record of an epoch fondly
gazed back upon, when—

"He made peace in the land,
　And Israel rejoiced with great joy.
And each sat under his vine and his fig-tree,
　And there was none to make them afraid;
And no one was left in the land to fight them,
　And the kings were discomfited in those days."
(XIV. 11.)

Note —There is an edition of 1 Maccabees with notes in
the *Cambridge Bible for Schools*, by Fairweather and Black,
and of 1 and 2 Maccabees in the *Temple Apocrypha* (Dent),
by Fairweather.

II. MACCABEES

THE Second Book of Maccabees is not a continuation of the first. It is a parallel account covering nearly the same ground. It is "alius non secundus," as Luther says. Its record being from 175 B.C. to 161 B C., the beginning is most valuable, as treating a short period before the accession of Antiochus of which we have no other account but that of Josephus. It claims to be an epitome of a long history in five books by a certain Jason of Cyrene. The writer professes to aim at broadness of treatment, brevity, and attractiveness in his choice of excerpts, and in his summarizing. The result is an obvious want of unity in the book, and a style that is somewhat haphazard and sensational. Jason's book, of which we know nothing beyond what this writer tells us, seems to have been written shortly after the close of the Maccabæan struggle between 120 B C and 110 B.C. " Its author," Professor Torrey says,[1] " was a contemporary of men who had taken part in the Maccabæan struggle." And he concludes that he depended on oral accounts at second hand, while he was not blessed with a very strong critical or literary faculty. The writer prefixes to his history two letters said to have been sent by the Jews of Palestine to the dispersed among the Gentiles, the one dated 143 B C , the other 124 B.C., urging them to keep the newly established Feast of Dedication. There seems no valid reason to reject these documents altogether, though they are probably summarized and altered.

He also writes a preface (ii. 19–32), explaining his method and objects, and concludes with a short

[1] *Encycl. Bib* , III. 2870.

epilogue (xv. 37–39). He opens by relating how Helio-
dorus, the Chancellor of Antiochus, sent to seize the
Temple treasures, was deterred by a miraculous vision
(iii. 1–39), and describes the sordid intrigues of Simon
and Jason for the High Priesthood, the Hellenic
innovations among the Jews, the plundering of Jerusalem, the martydom of Eleazar and a mother and
her seven sons, the early successes of Judas, Antiochus'
death, and the purification of Jerusalem, with the
Hanukka Feast. Then follow the further successes of
Judas, with angelic help, a three years' peace followed by Nicanor's renewed attack, defeat and death,
and the Institution of the Feast of Dedication.

When we compare this with 1 Maccabees we see that
the writer differs fundamentally in object and tone
of mind. He is bent on glorifying the Jews at all
costs, and is specially interested in the Temple, the
Priesthood, and the promotion of the new Feast of
Dedication, which is the climax of his story. He
draws out the constancy of the Jews not by a vivid
unfolding of events, but by sensational accounts of
torture and martyrdoms. He depends much on the
supernatural, and attributes the success of Judas
to angelic help, rather than to his own heroic spirit.
1 Maccabees is far more to be trusted, when the statements of the two writers conflict, as they very often do
in their parallel narratives. And yet 2 Maccabees
must not be considered to be without historical value.
There are passages which, by their graphic details,
seem to bring us nearer to the actual events than the
more sober and literary manner of the other writer.

The writer's advanced teaching on the resurrection
is noticeable : " There is no other pre-Christian Jewish
book which puts forth the doctrine of the resurrection
of the body more definitely." [1] And we have, too, the
interesting account and comment on Judas's sacrifices
and prayers for the dead (xii. 43–45) : " For if he
were not expecting that the fallen would rise again it
would have been superfluous and useless to pray for the

[1] Oesterley, p 489

dead. And if he in doing this was looking for the splendour of the gracious reward which is laid up for them that have fallen asleep in godliness, holy and pious was the thought. Wherefore he made a propitiation for them that had died that they might be released from their sin "

The writer's attitude to the supernatural, and such teaching as the above on the resurrection and prayers for the dead are the only guide to the date of the epitome. He seems to regard what he says as the normal teaching, well known and acceptable to those to whom it was addressed This would make it considerably later than 1 Maccabees. Scholars are agreed in placing it some time before the beginning of the Christian era.

It seems to have influenced Hebrews xi 35–38, where we have a reproduction of the Greek of 2 Maccabees vi. and vii. and x. 6.

III. MACCABEES

THIS book has no connection with the Maccabæan struggle. We can only conjecture why it was classed with the Maccabæan books. It was probably written about 100 B.C at the same period as the Letter of Aristeas and 2 Maccabees, with both of which it is linked by literary similarity.

Its writer was, in all probability, an orthodox Jew of Alexandria, loyal to the Temple and the Law, and untouched by Hellenistic influences. He adopts a pseudo-classical style, artificial and bombastic, using a number of strange and original words. He does not refer to apocalyptic ideas, or the Messiah, or the hope of a future life, but belongs to the strict and more conservative school.

The incidents recorded are an attempt of King Ptolemy IV. (Philopator) after the Battle of Raphia in 217 B C. to enter the Temple at Jerusalem, his repulse by angels, and the revenge he takes on the Jews by degrading the Egyptian Jews, interfering with their religion, and letting loose elephants inflamed by strong drink upon a Jewish concourse in the Hipprodrome at Alexandria. An angelic vision turns the elephants against the Egyptian persecutors, and the King repents, and becomes friendly to the Jews.

Now although this chain of incidents is obviously unhistorical, as it stands, there is no doubt a foundation of truth in the different parts of the story Let us see what it is.

The writer differs in detail in his account of the Battle of Raphia from that of the historian Polybius, and he is thought to follow the more popular work

of a certain Ptolemy of Megalopolis, who dealt largely
in the extravagant and marvellous, and designedly
blackened the character of Philopator.

In Josephus (*contra Ap*. ii. 5) we have a similar
story of drunken elephants, let loose by Physcon
(Ptolemy IX., 146–117 B C.) on the Alexandrian Jews,
who supported his sister Cleopatra in her claim to
the throne, which turn and attack his followers.
Josephus also mentions in the same chapter a visit
of Ptolemy Euergetes I. to the Jewish Temple to offer
thanksgiving, in which similar events happen to those
recorded in 3 Maccabees.

It seems likely that behind these references of
Josephus lie the actual historical circumstances,
which the writer connects together in a new order,
to suit his own purpose.

This purpose is, of course, similar to that of the
writers of Esther and Daniel—the glorification of the
Jewish race and their religion, and the stiffening of their
fibre by the contemplation of what had presumably
happened in the past to their own faithful members,
and to all who had ventured to persecute them. It
had, too, a reference to the educated Jewish world:
it was meant to lead them to imply that the Jewish
race had a peculiar sanctity, and that it was danger-
ous to interfere with them; while, by the way, it
emphasized the thorough loyalty of the Jews to the
Ptolemies, so long as they were treated with justice
and consideration.

The book is only interesting as throwing a light on
the feeling of the Jews at this period to their Egyptian
conquerors.

Note —This book is most accessible in Charles's *Apocrypha
and Pseudepigrapha*, Vol I, and in S.P C.K. Texts, 3 and
4 Maccabees   C. W. Emmet.

THE BOOK OF TOBIT

WE may call the Book of Tobit an historical novel, if we lay stress on "novel" rather than "historical." The writer's object was not to write history, but to point spiritual and moral lessons with an historical background. That background is vague, false, and full of anachronisms. It is better to call it a story with a purpose, or several purposes

The writer, whom most English scholars recognize as a Jew living in Egypt somewhere between 300 and 200 B C. (after the return from captivity, and before the Maccabæan revolt), in close touch with the Persian influences which were very strong in Egypt in the third century B C., wrote his book partly to counteract forces hostile to Judaism, and partly—for he was a born story-teller—from the story-telling instinct. In it we find most artistically blended the various streams that would affect the mental life of a pious Jew of liberal tendencies living in Egypt removed from the politics and narrowing ecclesiasticism of the Jerusalem of the Return. The writer yields to none in his reverence for the Law, the performance of the duties to the Temple, and in love of the Holy City. One of his objects is to protest against violations of the purity of Jewish marriage, another to put in the forefront the duty of burying the dead. He is profoundly impressed with the need of a right spirit in prayer and almsgiving—and gives examples of very beautiful praying   He paints his characters in the quiet light and shade of the domesticity of the patriarchal age, drawn from the Book of Genesis   But Jewish sources are but a tithe of what lies behind Tobit. We can trace the presence of at least three non-Jewish stories, which are worked in: namely, the Story of Ahikar, the Tale of the Grateful Dead Man, and the story told in the Tractate of Khons. Ahikar, indeed, is made a relative of Tobit. His story, which appears in many forms, is the tale of the adopted son, who betrays his benefactor, and eventually is punished. The next tale relates how a traveller stays to bury a dead body, and on arriving at his destination falls in love with a rich lady. On the marriage night a serpent-demon springs out of her mouth to slay him, and is put to flight by the spirit of the buried man, who was her husband. And the Tractate of Khons, a propagandist document preserved on a stele, is a similar story of a princess cured of a demon through an emissary from the Egyptian God Khons.

The writer of Tobit was also in a circle of ideas of more definite angelic mediation than that of the Old Testament. His race had no doubt reached this through contact with Persia, together with the magical ideas that are also prominent in his book

He opens with Tobit's narrative of his being carried to Nineveh in the days of Shalmaneser, with his wife and son Tobias. He tells of his loyalty to the Law, his almsgiving, and his care to bury the bodies of the dead in his captivity. It was after contracting defilement through one of these good actions, that he lay in the courtyard, and the droppings of the sparrows blinded him. The scene then changes to Ecbatana in Media, where Sarah, the daughter of Raguel, is under the influence of the demon Asmodeus, the slayer of seven men in succession who have aspired to be her husband. The Angel Raphael is sent down to accompany Tobias to Sarah, to make her his wife, and to recover a large sum of money deposited by Tobit. On the journey Tobias is attacked by a great fish in the river, which he brings to land with Raphael's aid; and he is told to keep the gall, liver, and heart, for the two latter when burned make a smoke that will drive away demons, while the gall will cure diseases of the eye. On their arrival the marriage

is arranged, Tobias burns the fish's liver and heart
in the marriage chamber, the demon is driven away
for ever, and the grave that Raguel has prepared for
another would-be son-in-law has to be filled up. The
money-deposit is received intact, and the party return
to Nineveh, where Tobias applies the gall of the fish
to his father's eyes and cures him. The book concludes
with the final words of Raphael to Tobit, and an
account of his Ascension, the prayer of Tobit, and his
last words. Such is a bald summary of the course
of the story, which by the simple skill of the writer
in artistically uniting the domestic, the moral, the
religious, and the marvellous has charmed the ears of
Jew and Christian alike through the two thousand
years of its life.

The writer's leading religious ideas are similar to
those of Ben-Sira, who belonged to the same epoch.
Both have the same teaching about the worship and
offerings to the Temple; both teach the efficacy of
almsgiving, and of prayer, though in Tobit fasting
is not dwelt on; both are equally dumb as to the
possibilities of a resurrection; while both are nobly
universalistic in their outlook on the Messianic age,
for example—

" A bright light shall shine unto the ends of the
    earth.
  Many nations shall come from afar,
And the inhabitants of the utmost ends of the earth
    unto thy holy name."

                                 (XIII. 11.)

With regard to the influence of this book on the
New Testament, there is no doubt that it acted constantly with the force of a set of ideas that had by
their artistic presentment worked itself into the minds
of cultured and uncultured alike. In idea and turn
of phrase Tobit is always reappearing in the New
Testament. In his teaching on prayer and almsgiving
Our Lord reproduces and spiritualizes what Tobit had

said. There are many instances in St. Paul's Epistles which show that he must have been very familiar with the book. And the demonic part of Tobit has close analogies with Rev. xx. 2 and xxi. 10–21, as has also the description of the New Jerusalem (Tobit xiii. 16–18) :

" The gates of Jerusalem shall be builded with sapphire
    and emerald,
  And all thy walls with precious stones.
The towers of Jerusalem shall be builded with gold,
  And their battlements with pure gold.
The streets of Jerusalem shall be paved
  With carbuncles and stones of Ophir ;
And the gates of Jerusalem shall utter hymns of
    gladness,
  And all her houses shall say, Halleluiah."

Moreover one cannot fail to recognize the verbal similarities between the account of Raphael's Ascension (Tobit xii. 16–22) and the Gospel narratives of the Transfiguration, Resurrection, and Ascension of our Lord There were of course other "Ascensions" recounted in the apocryphal writings, and probably the writer of Tobit is using the set forms of words associated with such descriptions. The writers of the Gospels used naturally the same turns of phrase in describing in popular language events of the same outward character, but of incomparably greater significance, in the Gospel story.

Note.—The *Temple* edition (Dent), edited by Sayce, with Judith and the Additions to Daniel

THE BOOK OF JUDITH

LIKE Tobit, the Book of Judith is a historical romance, in which dates, historical characters and events are used somewhat at random to afford a picturesque setting for the unfolding of great national and religious ideals. It was evidently written at a time of trial, perhaps during the Maccabæan revolt, to stiffen the courage of the people. The writer was of the Pharisaic party, and wrote in Hebrew, from which our Greek versions must all have been translated. He had full knowledge of his own sacred books, and shows considerable literary skill in working up to the climax of his story. If the " Song of Judith " is really part of the original book, and not an earlier writing incorporated by the writer, he was also a man of the deepest spiritual insight and poetic feelings.

With regard to the historical setting the story is placed in the time of " Nebuchadnezzar, King of Nineveh," who died in the year 562 B.C., and who is regarded as sending his expedition after the return of the Jews from captivity, at the earliest 536 B C. Nebuchadnezzar did not reign at Nineveh, nor attack Media, nor capture Ecbatana, as here represented. Various attempts have been made to find some historical personage who may be disguised under the name of Nebuchadnezzar. The historical framework seems most likely to have been suggested by the campaign of Artaxerxes Ochus, King of Persia, against Phœnicia and Egypt, though there is no historical confirmation in any records of anything corresponding to the events of the Book of Judith. This campaign took place about 350 B.C., and there was a Holofernes, who is stated

to have died in his own country, and a Bagoas concerned in it (Diodorus Siculus, xxxi. 19; xvi. 47)

The problem must remain insoluble, why the writer
should misname this monarch, or whether he was
intentionally disguising the names of persons of his
own day. But the real interest of the Book of Judith
does not turn on the accuracy of the writer's historical
knowledge. Nor would it be increased if it could be
proved to be, as some have thought, a romance
founded on a local legend, which had a kernel of actual
truth   Its real interest lies in the extremely dramatic
figure of the heroine, and the vigorous enunciation
from her lips of the faith and practice of the Jewish
race. And it is also a remarkable presentment of
the views of the typically Pharisaic party before their
final crystallization into hidebound legalism.

The first seven of the sixteen chapters are intro-
ductory, and relate how Nebuchadnezzar sends a
punitive expedition under Holofernes of 120,000
infantry and 12,000 cavalry to chastise Syria and
Egypt for not joining him in a war against Media.
Arriving at Esdraelon he finds the Jews of Bethulia
(a rocky fortress-town which may be Shechem) have
stopped the passes leading to Jerusalem. Achior, an
Ammonite, tells him that the Jews can only be con-
quered if they offend their God, and as a punishment
for his impertinence is handed over to the enemy
Holofernes gets possession of Bethulia's water-supply
and sits down to starve the Jews out. After thirty-
four days it is determined by the besieged that the
town shall only hold out for five more days.

In the eighth chapter the rich widow Judith appears
from her retirement, and proposes to go and work a
deliverance. With a maid, bearing " clean food,"
she is admitted to the presence of Holofernes, and
assures him that the Jews are about to incur God's
anger by eating the sacred food, and that she would
inform him the moment they could be safely attacked.
For three nights she is allowed to go outside the camp
for prayer, but on the fourth she consents to go to

Holofernes' feast. He drinks much more wine than he had drunk at any time in one day since he was born, while Judith partakes only of her own food. The servants depart and leave them together, and Judith after prayer takes Holofernes' sword, " and smote twice upon his head with all her might, and she took away his head from him, and tumbled his body down from the pillars; and anon after she went forth, and gave Holofernes his head to her maid; and she put it in her bag of meat." They escape to Bethulia, and are received with joy. The Jews make a sortie, and the enemy attempt to rouse Holofernes, and discovering what has been done, flee in disorder.

The last chapter contains Judith's beautiful song of praise—

" For their mighty one did not fall by young men,
  Neither did sons of the Titans smite him,
  Nor did high giants set upon him;
  But Judith the daughter of Merari made him weak
    with the beauty of her countenance."

(XVI 7)

Though the book was not received in the Canon, it is mentioned in the Liturgy for the Feast of Dedication, founded by Judas Maccabæus. It was quoted by Clement of Rome, and most of the early Fathers, and was a favourite subject for Art in the Middle Ages.

Its Pharisaic character is very evident Obedience to the law is the essence of righteousness, and the secret of a good conscience. Judith observes not only the feasts, but their eves; she is careful not to eat forbidden food; she fasts constantly. She teaches that God will punish disobedience to these ritual ordinances not only here but hereafter.

THE BOOK OF SIRACH

" ECCLESIASTICUS " is the name in the English Bible
for the book whose original title was probably
" The Wisdom of Jesus Ben-Sira."   " Ecclesiasticus "
means " the Church Book," and the name dates from
the fourth century A D , when it was regarded as a
useful book of instruction for catechumens.

Ben-Sira wrote in Hebrew somewhere about the
year 175 B.C.   And his book, as the Prologue tells
us, was translated into Greek by his grandson at
Alexandria probably in the year 132 B.C.   The
Hebrew original had been lost since the eleventh
century, and the discovery of the greater part of it
sheet by sheet, in the Genizah at Cairo by Prof.
Schechter and others from the year 1896 onwards,
is among the romances of modern research.   As
might be expected, there are considerable differences
between the Hebrew and the Greek, both having
passed through many copyings and editions.

The book belongs to the Wisdom [Hokmah]
Literature of the Jews, which was the proverbial
philosophy, or commentary on life and duty, that
naturally developed out of the homely sayings and
fables that seem from the early books of the Old
Testament to have been as common among the Jews
as among other peoples.   In the time of Jeremiah
the specifically wise man or ethical student and teacher
stood with the priest and the prophet as one of the
leaders of the religious life of the Jews   (Jer. xviii. 18).
The Hebrew mind realized that all Wisdom came to
man from God, both the knowledge of God Himself,
and the wisdom of ordinary practical life.   The
wisdom-writers loved to paint Wisdom as a personal

being in the company of God from the beginning,
and sent by Him to holy souls. The attainment of
it depended on human effort and concentration;
earnestness in its pursuit was always rewarded, but
its growth in the community required a leisured class
wholly devoted to its cultivation.

From the time of Alexander the Great the Jews
had been affected by Greek culture, and had learned
to make wisdom or knowledge the root-principle of
virtue. As " virtue " to the Hebrew could only mean
obedience to the divinely given Law, we can see how
he was forced to identify the true wisdom ultimately
with the Law, and to say " the fear of the Lord is
the consummation of Wisdom." Thus in his pursuit
of Wisdom, unlike the Greek thinkers, he was in a
sense searching for something, the main outlines of
which were already known to him. He always comes
back to the precepts of the Law. Of this literature
of practical philosophy, Ben-Sira proclaims himself
a humble and belated follower. He comes " last of
all, as one that gleaneth after the grape-gatherers."
But he has filled his wine-press. And the stream he
led into his garden to irrigate it has become a river,
and the river a sea. He has developed to the full
the hints of the Proverbs and the Psalms for the
guidance of his own day. Thus his book became a
comprehensive guide of life in every particular. It
explores with the reserve of his Sadducæan limitations
the deep questions of sin and freewill, death and
retribution. It lays down rules for tactful behaviour
in the Council, in the market and at home. It teaches
care and circumspection in men's relation with women,
and with associates in business. It includes detailed
advice on behaviour in society and at the dinner-
table. Its writer is evidently one who has travelled
and figured in the highest society of his day; he is
no mere student cut off from the experience of life.
" Relishing a good table, music and congenial company, but moderate in his enjoyments; genuinely
pious, and a constant reader of holy books, but not

given to enthusiasm, and free from superstitions."
In the Book of Sirach, as in Montaigne or Bacon, there
is always the charm of following one who thoroughly
knows his way through the beaten tracks of human
nature.

As Ben-Sira lived before the Pharisee and the
Sadducee had definitely diverged we do not find in
his teaching the hard-and-fast lines of the partisan.
Yet there is no doubt that he was in essence a Sadducee. He insists on the Law of Moses, not on any
oral ordinances, as the rule of duty; he has little
room for the hope of a Messiah; he has no belief in a
conscious life after death. In all this he agrees more
with the Sadducees, as well as in his tolerant attitude
towards the Greek world, in spite of his programme
to show the superiority of Jewish over Hellenic wisdom

The Book of Sirach must have been well known
to the writers of the New Testament   There are
significant parallels between the Language of the
Gospel and Sirach; the following have been noted—

Matt. vi. 14	.	.	. Sirach xxviii. 2
Matt. vi. 19 *seq*	.	.	. Sirach xxix 12
Matt. xvi. 27	.	.	. Sirach xxxii. 24
Luke i. 17 .	.	.	. Sirach xlviii. 10
Luke xii 15 *seq.* ⎱	.	.	⎰ Sirach xxxi. 3
(The Rich Fool) ⎰			⎱ and xi 18–19.

But the Epistle of St. James shows actual and
close dependence—*e. g* cf. Jas. 1 2–4: "Count it all
joy, my brethren," etc , with Sirach ii. 1: "My son,
if thou comest to serve the Lord, prepare thy soul
for temptation." And Jas. 1–19: "Let every man
be swift to hear, slow to speak," with Sirach v. 11:
"Be swift to hear." And note also—

James i. 5	.	.	. Sirach xviii. 18.
James i. 6–8	.	.	. Sirach i. 28.
James i. 13–15	.	.	. Sirach xv. 11–20.
James i. 23	.	.	. Sirach xii. 11.
James v. 5	.	.	. Sirach xxvii. 10.
James v. 14	.	.	. Sirach xxxviii. 9–15.

It will be acknowledged, too, that Ben-Sira's recognition of the value of sacrifice only on its ethical, not on its *ex opere operato* side, in its high spiritual tone is in full accord with the teaching of the New Testament. He could write in the manner of the great prophets—

" The sacrifice of the unrighteous man is a mocking offering,
And unacceptable are the oblations of the godless.
The Most High hath no pleasure in the offerings of the ungodly,
Neither doth He forgive sins for a multitude of sacrifices."

(XXXIV. 18.)

Note.—The S P C K edition, by Oesterley. 1916.

THE WISDOM OF SOLOMON

THE Book of the Wisdom of Solomon is generally ascribed to a Jew of Alexandria, as it blends Greek and Hebrew thought in the manner of Philo. There are writers, however, who maintain that it was written in Palestine. It falls naturally into two divisions, which are so different in manner and purpose that, as we shall see, it is almost certainly a work of a composite character, its component parts being of different dates. The first part, if this be so, would probably be dated from 50 B C. to 30 B.C., the second some twenty years later. It should be said, however, that important scholars place it from fifty to sixty years earlier

Its ascription to Solomon was seen as early as the time of Jerome to be only a literary device, and there are many indications that the name was adopted because the book was intended to be a corrective of the materialistic and pessimistic teaching of Ecclesiastes, also ascribed to Solomon.

The first part of the book extends to xi. 1, and includes (a) a mass of eschatological teaching on the destiny of the righteous and the wicked, and (b) the praise of Wisdom, which gives its name to the book. Its teaching is as follows : Wisdom cannot co-exist with sin, purity of life is the only road to knowledge of God. The sinner will not ultimately escape punishment, for there is " an ear of jealousy which listeneth to all things." The world is inherently healthy, " God made not death," it is men that bring punishment on themselves. The pessimist and the sensualist are both wrong . those who say, " Short and sorrowful is our life, by mere chance were we born," and those who cry, "Let us crown ourselves with rosebuds, before they wither," and do not hesitate to oppress the poor and helpless. Their victims will be justified and avenged, for "the souls of the righteous are in the hand of the Lord, and there shall no torment touch them," whereas the ungodly shall suffer both themselves and in the persons of their descendants; their remorse at the Judgement will be bitter when they cry, "What did our arrogancy profit us?" The following of Wisdom is most incumbent on the great, for "mighty men shall be searched out mightily" (vi. 5). Then begins the panegyric of Wisdom.

She "is radiant and fadeth not away, and easily is she beheld of them that love her." "She forestalleth them that desire *to know her*, making herself first known." She came to Solomon in answer to prayer, and she is his chief treasure, and the source of all his knowledge. "She is a breath of the power of God, and a clear effluence of the glory of the Almighty . . . from generation to generation passing into holy souls, she maketh them friends of God and prophets." She becomes more and more a personal being as the writer proceeds; she is the bride Solomon desired, being enamoured of her beauty; she alone can be his teacher, prophet, and friend, she who is not weighed down with the corruption of the body, nor subject to mortal weakness. Her work in history is recounted from Adam to Moses: she ever guided, and "prospered their works by the hand of a holy prophet" (xi. 1).

Here we pass to the second part of the book, which is of a much more prosaic character: "We have no longer a poem extolling goodness and celebrating Wisdom, but a Midrash in glorification of the Jews." Chapters xi. to xix contrast the lot of Israel in their flight in the wilderness with that of Egypt beset by the plagues.

Chapters xiii. to xv. are a digression on the evil of idolatry. In the spirit of Isaiah xl. it is the height

of folly to worship a piece of wood not good enough
for the shipbuilder.   In conclusion, the writer shows
how the elements by their transmutation ruined the
Egyptians and defended the Israelites, " for the world
fighteth for the righteous," and—

" . . . the creation, ministering to thee its maker,
  Straineth its force against the unrighteous for
    punishment,
  And slackeneth it, in behalf of them that trust in
    thee, for beneficence."   (XVI. 24.)

Thus in the miraculous story of the Exodus the
writer sees a change effecting itself under the surface
of outward nature, making for moral ends.   Fire
forgot to burn, and water to quench.

" For the elements changed their order one with
    another,
  Just as the notes of a psaltery vary the character
    of the rhythm."   (XIX 18)

Such being a brief abstract of Wisdom, it will be
plain that it had certain and definite objects, that
it was written emphatically for a purpose : that
purpose was to recall the Jews of the Dispersion,
constantly in danger of succumbing to the materialism,
scepticism, and idolatry of the environment of
Hellenism, back to the simplicity and purity of their
ancestral faith.   Life, because it was short, was not
to be squandered in vain pleasures ; problems of God
and man, hard though they might be, could be solved
by patient study of the Jewish records ; and after
their long vicissitudes it would be shameful indeed
because of persecution to go over to idolatry.   These
warnings must have been only too much needed by
the Jews of a city like Alexandria.
There is little doubt that Wisdom had a considerable influence on the writers of the New Testament,
and especially on St. Paul and St John.   Thackeray
thinks that the former must have made " a close

study of it," and traces the result in the Pauline teaching on idolatry, predestination, and eschatology.

A comparison of one or two typical similarities will be interesting.

Wisdom ii. 24. By the envy of the devil death entered into the world	Rom. v. 12. . . . Sin entered into the world, and death through sin.
Wisdom iii 8. The righteous shall judge nations, and have dominion over peoples.	1 Cor. vi. 2, 3 Or know ye not that the saints shall judge the world— etc.
Wisdom v. 17–20. He shall take his jealousy as complete armour [*panoply*]. He shall put on righteousness as a breastplate, and shall take judgement as a helmet; He shall take holiness as an invincible shield, And shall sharpen stern wrath as a sword.	Eph. vi. 11–20. Put on the whole armour of God [*panoply*] —etc. [Both passages are, of course, founded on Isa. lix. 17.]
Wisdom ix. 5. For a corruptible body weigheth down the soul, and the earthly frame lieth heavy on the mind that is full of cares.	2 Cor. v. 1. For we know that if the earthly house of our tabernacle . . .; and v. 4. We that are in this tabernacle do groan, being burdened.

The number of such parallels, though no single one is conclusive by itself, seems to prove St. Paul's absorption of the ideas of Wisdom.

It will perhaps be asked, as the sublime figure of Wisdom, the agent of God in creation and the revealer of the mind of God, stands unveiled before us, what did the writer exactly intend her to be? Is she a " person "? Is she an attribute of God poetically personified? The answer with regard to this Jewish personification of Wisdom, which occurs also in

Prov. viii and Sirach xxiv., is that the idea of personality was not at all clearly developed at that time,
and that the Oriental mind was and is far more
prone to vague and poetic imagination than ours.
Thus the nation was to the prophet a bride, or a
despoiled mother, and the stars and powers of nature
were confused with angelic personalities. There was
far more of poetry in the personification of Wisdom
than of philosophical exactness But even we can
feel something of the grandeur and beauty of the
conception of a personal element entering in as the
special inspiration of the ideals that uplift and
inspire mankind.

Note —Edited by Gregg, in the *Cambridge Bible for Schools.*
(1909) S P C K Text.   Oesterley

I. BARUCH AND THE EPISTLE OF JEREMIAH

THE Book of Baruch of our official Apocrypha claims to have been written by Baruch, the secretary of the prophet Jeremiah, during the captivity in Babylon. After having been read there, the preface says it was sent to Jerusalem with a sum of money for the expenses of sacrifices, with a request that the Jews should pray for Nebuchadnezzar and his son Belshazzar.

This would have been, according to 1. 2 (" the fifth year "), either 592 B.C. or 582 B C. But there is little doubt among scholars that it was really written quite six centuries and a half later, that is to say, near the time of the fall of Jerusalem, A D. 70. In this case the events and characters of the time of the Babylonian exile are used to refer to the present. Rome is Babylon, Nebuchadnezzar is Vespasian, and the writer, continuing the blunder in the Book of Daniel, makes Belshazzar the son of Nebuchadnezzar, and so by him means Titus, son of Vespasian.

But as the Book of Baruch is really not a single book, but three books bound together, each requires separate treatment.

Baruch consists of—

(i) The Book of Confessions (i.–iii 8);
(ii) A fragment of " Wisdom " literature (iii 9–iv. 4); and
(iii) A prophetic encouragement (iv. 5–v. 9)

(i) The Confession acknowledges that the Exile is God's punishment of Israel's disobedience, and refusal to obey Jeremiah and serve Nebuchadnezzar. A promise of restoration and rule over Palestine is given. This is all in agreement with the Pharisaic

I. BARUCH AND EPISTLE OF JEREMIAH 39

attitude of complete submission to Rome (Jos *Bell Jud* vi. 3, 4, and ix. 2, 3), and we shall be right in referring this portion to A.D. 75. Dr. Oesterley[1] dwells on a striking similarity between this and passages of the Jewish Prayer Book, especially the identity of the order and phrasing of petitions in the " Eighteen Benedictions " (*Shemoneh Esreh*). He would conclude that i. 15–iii. 8 is an expansion of some part of the Temple Liturgy of the first century A D

(ii) This section (written in verse) dwells on the common topic of the Wisdom Literature ; God's " *Law* " is Wisdom · it is nowhere else but in Him. He has committed it to the Jews. The neglect of it is the cause of their downfall   Let them lay hold of it, and walk in its light. It is referred to the beginning of the second century, and was probably written in some Jewish college in Babylonia, where the faith of the chosen people was fed and nourished by study

(iii) We pass to a prophetic passage, reminiscent of the second Isaiah. Jerusalem encourages her children in their affliction, and prophesies a new dawn. This is succeeded by a message of cheer from God to her, which is almost identical with the eleventh of the Psalms of Solomon, probably written about 50 B C., *i. e* about a hundred and fifty years before, since it seems to reflect a period of peace, for it runs—

" . . God hath appointed that every high mountain, and the everlasting hills, should be made low,
And the valleys filled up to make plain the road,
That Israel may go safely in the glory of God.
Moreover the woods and every sweet-smelling tree have overshadowed Israel,
For God shall lead Israel with joy in the light of His glory,
With the mercy and righteousness that cometh from Him."   (V. 7–9.)

[1] Oesterley, p 500.

The Epistle of Jeremiah

The seventy-three verses of this Epistle are joined on to Baruch in the Vulgate, but the Septuagint places them after Lamentations, under a separate title.

It is directed against the danger of idolatry, and recalls such passages as Jer. x. 1–16 and Isa. xlix 9–19.

It is not at all easy to date it   As unfaithfulness usually attacked Israel in days of peace and prosperity, there is a presumption against its having been written either during the Maccabæan struggle, or the war that ended in the fall of Jerusalem.   Thus we may either place it in the time of John Hyrcanus (*circa* 110 B C.), or a hundred years later.   In contrast to such conclusions we have the opinion of Prof. C. J Ball that it is the translation of a Hebrew original, produced to counteract the actual danger of Jews in Babylon adopting idolatry about 306 B.C.

Note —Edition in *Temple Apocrypha* (Dent).

THE PRAYER OF MANASSES

MANASSES, in 2 Chron. xxxiii 12 *seq* , is the typical penitent. He has exceeded the Jewish kings in wickedness; he is punished, repents, and is restored to his kingdom. Both in verses 12–13 and 18–19 the chronicler tells us that he " prayed." It was natural, therefore, that a prayer should appear in later days purporting to be his. Whether the prayer that bears his name was a penitential psalm of a general character that became identified with his name, or whether it was actually written by some pious Jew as " the Prayer of Manasses," it is difficult to decide. " *I have set up abominations and have multiplied detestable things,*" if it is an original verse of the Prayer, would seem to make the latter opinion the most probable, referring to his enormities as related in 2 Chron. xxxiii 6.

The prayer is preserved in the Christian second or third century writing known as the *Didascalia*, which forms the first six books of the *Apostolical Constitutions*, compiled not later than the sixth century. It is there given to illustrate the power of repentance, and the depth of God's mercy. It consists of fifteen verses, and includes Invocation of God (1–7), Confession of Sin (8–10), Plea for Forgiveness (11–15). " The prayer," says Dr. Oesterley,[1] " is a beautiful one, finely constructed, full without being drawn out, and breathing throughout deep personal religion It is certainly one of the best pieces in the Apocrypha." It is probable that it was written about the beginning of the first century B C

[1] Oesterley, p 404

ADDITIONS TO THE BOOK OF DANIEL

I.—THE PRAYER OF AZARIAH AND THE SONG OF THE THREE CHILDREN

THIS block of literary matter appears in all the Greek MSS. of the Book of Daniel between vv. 23 and 24 of chapter iii. It does not occur in the Aramaic text. In the A.V. and R.V. it is headed "'The Song of the Three Holy Children,' which followed in the third chapter of Daniel after this place—*fell down bound into the midst of the burning fiery furnace* (ver. 23). That which followeth is not in the Hebrew, to wit, *And they walked*—unto these words, *Then Nebuchadnezzar* (ver 24)"

As the ordinary text shows no reason why Nebuchadnezzar should be " astonished," it seems obvious that this long interpolation has taken the place of something similar, which has been lost from the Hebrew.

The passage divides itself under analysis into two pieces of narrative, the Prayer of Azariah, and the Song of the Three Children. The first piece of narrative (vv. 1 and 2) links it on to the context, the second relates the heating of the furnace, the burning of the attendants, and the descent of the Angel of the Lord.

The prayer acknowledges the justice of God's judgements on Jerusalem, bewails the cruelty and wickedness of her enemy, recalls the promises made to Abraham, Isaac and Jacob, and describes the forlorn state of the Jews, " without prince, or prophet, or leader, or burnt-offering, or sacrifice, or oblation, or incense, or place to offer before Thee and to find mercy." In return for penitence it asks for restoration and judgement on the enemy

The song with its refrain, " *Sing and highly exalt Him for ever*," is the *Benedicite* of the Prayer Book, with a Preface of Blessing, and an ascription. In its joyous note of union in the worship of God with all things created there is a great contrast to the depressed tone of the prayer which precedes it. And indeed there seems no reason why the two should be linked together. Both compositions seem to have originally referred to events other than those recorded in Daniel. The name " Azariah " seems to be the reason of the inclusion of the prayer; the writer may well have been an Azariah of the time of the persecution of Antiochus. Had one of the children prayed thus he could hardly have described Jerusalem as " without a prophet " in the early days of the exile.

The Song, again, seems to be a psalm written in days of prosperity, when the Temple was the centre of worship Its presence in this context is an enigma

It would seem that the interpolator wished to connect the two ideas of national penitence and the glory of the Creator to comfort his countrymen under the stress of persecution, and selected these two compositions for the purpose.

II.—Susanna

It is practically certain that the scene of the story of Susanna was originally set in a township in Palestine, and that it had no connection with Daniel or Babylon in the days of the exile. Scholars are agreed that the original story bears every mark of having been written in the latter years of Alexander Jannæus, king and high-priest 103–76 B C., and that it was a tract intended to support the reform of the law, whereby the accused gained the benefit of cross-examination of witnesses   As we know that it was something of a burning question between Pharisees and Sadducees whether false witnesses should suffer death on the score of intention, or only in the event of their victims having been executed before the discovery of their fraud, the Pharisees holding the former and the Sadducees the latter view, we can well understand the *motif* of the story. The reform in the legal process is associated in the Mishna with the name of Simon ben Shetach, who, as the brother-in-law of Alexander, is supposed by Ball to have been instrumental in securing the triumph of the Pharisaic party (*Pirkē Aboth*, i. 9, Ball, *Wace*, ii 305–360)

It seems probable that a tradition of the story became involved in the Daniel-cycle, and the scene moved to the Babylon of three centuries before.

So far as the story is concerned, the Jewish tendency noticeable in the stories of Jael, Esther, and Judith to make a woman the means of deliverance again runs its course. It is well and dramatically told, and the characters stand out clearly. The simple issues of passion and purity, which are the abiding theme of romance, exercise their unfailing attraction

The story is familiar to all. The young wife of Joakim attracts the evil desire of his two friends, who were judges. They agree to surprise her together, and on so doing tell her that if she refuses to yield to them, they will accuse her of being unfaithful to her husband with a young man in the garden. She raises an alarm, and has no means of proving her innocence when accused. As she is being led out to die, a youth named Daniel stops them, and insists on the right of cross-examination. He questions the two accusers separately, and their accounts do not tally. They are, therefore, both gagged and hurled down a chasm

Such was the original story. It is plain that its transfer to Babylon only introduces impossible complications. The exiles could hardly have had pleasure gardens and hundreds of retainers, nor had Babylon a *stadium*, on which the interest of the tale partly turns It is fairly certain, too, that in the middle second century Daniel was a semi-angelic person, and could hardly have been treated of in the tone of this book. It was after the reform had been achieved that it became possible to add picturesque additions to what was at first a homely and useful parable Shakespeare's familiarity with the Apocrypha is shown in *The Merchant of Venice*, where Portia is a " A Daniel come to judgement."

III.—BEL AND THE DRAGON

In Bel and the Dragon we have the third addition appended to Daniel in the Greek and Latin versions. This was done because it gave illustrations of Daniel's wisdom and faith in the true God. Its origin was quite distinct, and it was translated from a Hebrew original, which has perished.

It is no doubt later than our Book of Daniel, which is usually placed 160 B C., and it was probably written in Palestine in a similar period of persecution to that which produced the longer book The reign of Antiochus VII. (139–128 B C) is suggested, as he followed the example of Antiochus Epiphanes in persecuting the Jewish religion

The book gives two distinct stories; the first, that of Bel, relates how Daniel, " who lived with the King, and was honoured among all his friends," refused to worship the image of the Babylonian God Bel or Marduk. We are not given any details of the worship, except the provision of large quantities of food and wine, that were left in the temple, and consumed during the night. By sprinkling ashes on the floor, Daniel proves that the priests and their families removed the victuals when the temple was closed, entering by secret doors. So the King has the image destroyed, and the priests killed

The story of the Dragon, founded on some serpent-worship at Babylon, or a tradition of such a cult, of which there is good evidence from inscriptions, tells how Daniel, refusing to bow down, claims that he will destroy the beast, in which the God is supposed to be. He therefore gives it a cake, composed of pitch, fat, and hair, which causes the serpent to burst asunder. As there is a popular outcry, Daniel is thrown into the den of lions, where he remains for seven days. He is miraculously fed by the prophet Habakkuk, who is transported by the hair of his head by the Angel of the Lord from Palestine, as he is on the way to his field taking his reapers their food. This incident seems to be a later excrescence. He is finally released, and his accusers, consigned to the den by the King, are devoured.

It seems best to regard this as simply a " snake " story, without any connection with the mythical " dragon " myth. There is considerable evidence for snake-worship at Babylon. The Greek δράκων is simply " snake," as is plain from Homer.

Bel and the Dragon does not throw much light on Hebrew religion, beyond the belief in a living God, as opposed to idolatry. The Habakkuk incident seems to show the demand for marvel, and descriptions of angelic mediation from those who found the story too tame and colourless.

Note.—Cf Daubeny: *The Three Additions to Daniel* 1906

ADDITIONS TO THE BOOK OF ESTHER

THE additions to the Book of Esther are six passages generally known by the first six letters of the alphabet, which were added to the Greek translation of Esther some time after it appeared in 114 B.C. In our A.V. and R.V., placed as they are together as an Appendix, their *motif* is less intelligible than in the Septuagint, where they are fitted naturally into the narrative. Their relegation to an Appendix was due to Jerome. They are the work of Hellenistic Jews of the same date as the Book of Wisdom, though, unlike Wisdom, their character is that of simple Jewish piety, unmixed with Alexandrian speculation. Their pious tone has suggested to some that they were intended to leaven a canonical book, which may have seemed of too secular a character, a book which does not once mention the name of God.

Their true position and contents are as follows—

A. [Before Esther i 1] Mordecai dreams of two great dragons, portending war. The righteous cry, and a small spring of water appears and grows into a great river. When he wakes he discovers the plot of two enemies against the King's life, and is promoted in consequence

B. [Between iii. 13 and iii. 14.] An imaginary copy of the letter of Artaxerxes, mentioned in Esther, iii. 13.

C. [After iv. 7.] The prayer of Mordecai, and the prayer of Esther: " Put eloquent speech into my mouth before the lion . . . save us by Thy hand, and help me who *stand* alone, and have none save Thee, O Lord."

D. [Follows C.] Describes Esther's appearance

before the King. " She herself was radiant in the perfection of her beauty, and her countenance was happy and lovely : but her heart was stricken with fear."

E. [Between viii. 12 and viii. 13] The letter of Artaxerxes annulling his former letter about the Jews.

F. [Concludes the book.] Mordecai's dream is interpreted. He and Haman were the two dragons, and Esther the spring that became a river. The concluding postscript, stating that the translation of Esther was brought to Egypt in the fourth year of Ptolemy and Cleopatra (*i. e.* 114 B C.) by " Dositheus, who said he was a priest and a Levite, and Ptolemæus his son," is generally regarded as authentic, but limited in its reference to the canonical book, not including the Additions

THE BOOK OF JUBILEES

OR "THE LITTLE GENESIS"

THE Book of Jubilees was written towards the end
of the reign of John Hyrcanus, the great Maccabæan
high priest and ruler, who inherited from his father
Simon, and defended by his energy and tact amid a
welter of contending powers around Palestine, the
prosperous and independent kingdom that had been
won by the indomitable spirit of his family. This
would mean that the book appeared some time
between 110 B C. and 105 B C., the year of John's
death, after a reign of twenty-nine years.

During his reign the position of the Jewish parties
had become fixed and determined, and the outstand-
ing event of his later years was his passing from the
ranks of the Pharisees to those of the Sadducees.
The reason given by Josephus for his desertion of
the Pharisees was that they had circulated scurrilous
stories about his legitimacy.

During his reign, too, there had been a continuous
Hellenistic influence upon Jewish thought and life,
no longer, of course, pressed by the sword of Seleucid
autocracy, but making its way by natural and
peaceful penetration.

We now know a great deal more about the standpoint of the two great Jewish parties than we did,
and are able to discount some of the statements of
Josephus with regard to them. We see better, too,
their attitude to the disintegrating forces of Hellenism.
We are learning to realize that the Sadducee was
not a characteristically worldly, sceptical, or irre-
ligious person, and that the Pharisee, so far from

D   49

seeking "separation" from the people, was the offspring of the people and the mouthpiece of their traditions. It was because the Sadducee was loyal to the Law as it stood that in rejecting the popular oral traditions he appeared cold and lacking in fervour. It was because he generally happened to be aristocratic that he came into more sympathetic touch with foreign culture. It was because the Pharisee believed in the inspiration of oral tradition, and the value of comments and Midrash accumulated by the wise, that he spoke more decidedly for Judaism undiluted by Hellenism, although he was no doubt to some extent unconsciously affected by non-Jewish ideas.

The Book of Jubilees is regarded by most scholars as a Pharisaic work, "the most triumphant manifesto of legalism." Yet there are some who think that it might have been worked over by a Sadducee, as the Sadducee was as loyal to the written law as the Pharisee.

The writer re-edits Genesis and Exodus from his own point of view. His object is to throw back the legal enactments of his religion into the earliest age, and to prove them to be bound up with the earliest revelation, unalterable, eternal. Thus the Jewish Feasts are observed by the Patriarchs, the angels submit to the rite of circumcision, and death is laid down as the universal penalty of breaking the Sabbath. The obligations of the Law are as real for heaven as earth; they are the special glory and crown of the Jew. Therefore they *must* have been made binding on the earliest ancestors of the Jewish race. And the lives of the Patriarchs under the guidance of the Law have to be purified as far as possible from offensive elements; thus Jacob is cleared from verbal falsehood by equivocation when he answers, "I am thy son," to Jacob's question, "Art thou my very son Esau?" All this is anti-Hellenistic; it buttresses the exclusive spirit of the Jewish race; it paints them as from the beginning admitted to the knowledge of the highest truth written in the heavenly tablets. What culture of Greece or Rome, what reasoning of philosopher or imagination of poet, could compete with this? The Jew had but to learn and follow the Law, and he was in possession of the ideal.

The literary interest of "Jubilees" lies in the large mass of Midrashic matter, which is incorporated into the story. It is always picturesque and quaint, and comes from many delightfully *naive* and child-like regions of thought and fancy. There is, too, a fine grandeur in the continuous insistence on the greatness of God, the certainty of His care, and the beauty of a simple obedience and trust. We have the curious Midrash when Adam leaves the garden : "And on that day was closed the mouth of all beasts, and of cattle, and of birds, and of whatever walks, and of whatever moves, so that they could no longer speak; for they had all spoken one with another with one lip and one tongue " (III. 28). As another example we may take this from the youth of Abraham : "And the seed-time came for the sowing of seed upon the land, and they all went forth to protect their seed against the ravens, and Abram went forth with those that went, and the child was a lad of fourteen years. And a cloud of ravens came to devour the seed, and Abram ran to meet them before they settled on the ground to devour the seed, and said . ' Descend not : return to the place whence ye came,' and they proceeded to turn back. And he caused the cloud of ravens to turn back that day seventy times, and of all the ravens throughout all the land where Abram was there settled there not so much as one. And all who were with him through-out all the land saw him cry out, and all the ravens turn back, and his name became great throughout all the land of the Chaldees. And there came to him this year all those that wished to sow, and he went with them till the time of sowing ceased ; and they sowed their land, and that year they brought enough grain home and ate and were satisfied. And in the

first year of the fifth week Abram taught those who
made implements for oxen, the artificers in wood,
and they made a vessel above the ground, facing
the frame of the plow, in order to put the seed therein,
and the seed fell down therefrom upon the share of
the plow, and was hidden in the earth, and they no
longer feared the ravens" (xi. 18–24).

The temptation of Abraham is regarded as similar
to that of Job. There were "voices in heaven"
attesting his love of God and faithfulness. Then
"the Prince Mastêmâ" came and suggested that he
would fail if tried by the command to sacrifice his
son.

"And the Lord knew that Abraham was faithful
in all his afflictions; for He had tried him through
his country and with famine, and had tried him with
the wealth of kings, and had tried him again through
his wife when she was torn from him, and with
circumcision; and had tried him through Ishmael
and Hagar when he sent them away. And in everything wherein He had tried him, he was found faithful, and his soul was not impatient, and he was not
slow to act; for he was faithful and a lover of the
Lord."

He thus describes the death of Abraham : "And
he placed two fingers of Jacob on his eyes, and he
blessed the God of gods, and he covered his face and
stretched out his feet, and slept the sleep of eternity,
and was gathered to his fathers. And notwithstand-
ing all this Jacob was lying in his bosom, and knew
not that Abraham his father was dead. And Jacob
awoke from his sleep, and beheld Abraham was cold
as ice, and he said : ' Father ! Father ! ' but there
was none that spoke. And he arose from his bosom,
and went and told Rebecca his mother; and Rebecca
went to Isaac his father in the night and told him;
and they went together, and Jacob with them, and
a lamp was in his hand, and when they had gone in
they found Abraham lying dead " (xxiii 1–5).

The reconciliation of Jacob and Esau by their

mother before her death is very beautifully told.
Esau swears that he will love him, and not desire
evil against him, but good only. But after Isaac's
death he appears in arms, and when Jacob rebukes
him for breaking his oath, he says, " Neither the
children of men nor the beasts of the earth have any
oath of righteousness which in swearing they have
sworn an oath valid for ever :

If the boar can change its skin, and make its bristles
    as soft as wool,
Or if it can cause horns to sprout forth on its head
    like a stag or sheep,
Then will I observe the tie of brotherhood with thee."

In the great battle that followed Jacob bends his
bow and shoots Esau with his own hand, and reduces
Edom to servitude.

The story of Joseph is not so fully told, nor the
life of Moses, with which the book ends.

Thus the book covers the story of Genesis and
Exodus from the Creation to the time of Moses, to
whom it is unfolded directly by the Angel of the
Presence on the Mount, and is remarkable for the
mass of detail that generations of pious thinkers had
blended with the original story, and for the evident
intention of the writer to exalt the law, to show the
superiority of the children of Jacob, and to assure
them of their great destiny.

Upon the last stage of this they had already
entered, and the advent of the Messiah who would
spring from the Jewish race was to be expected
in their own days. The author of Jubilees was not
alone in teaching that the Messianic era was closely
associated with the Maccabæan rule. Some had even
gone so far as to identify Simon or John Hyrcanus
with the Messiah. And indeed there was much in
the prosperity and vitality of the country which
seemed to fulfil the Old Testament prophecies. We
are here taught that it was to come without cataclysm

in a gradual and progressive human development. So the Angel of the Presence, after describing the enormities of Antiochus Epiphanes, and the horrors of the civil wars after 162 B.C., paints a time of reformation:

" And at that time the Lord will heal His servants,
And they shall rise up and see great peace,
And drive out their adversaries.
And the righteous shall see and be thankful,
And rejoice with joy for ever and ever,
And shall see all their judgements and curses upon their enemies,
And their bones shall rest in the earth,
And their spirits shall have much joy,
And they shall know that it is the Lord who executes judgement,
And shows mercy to thousands and thousands, and to all that love Him "   (XXIII. 30–32.)

A strongly Pharisaic element in the book is the prominence and activity of the spiritual world of angels and demons, and their nearness to the life of man   It is the Angel of the Presence who unfolds the revelation.   He and his compeers have it in their power to bind Mastêmâ, or Satan, the prince of the demons.   The angels were created on the first day with the heavens and the earth : " All the spirits which serve before Him—the angels of the presence, and the angels of sanctification, and the angels of fire, and the angels of the winds, and clouds, and darkness, and of snow, and of hail and of hoar-frost, and the angels of the voices and of the thunder and lightning, and of the spirits of cold and of heat "— in short, of all natural phenomena.   The demons are the spirits of the giants, who were the offspring of the heavenly watchers, sent down to instruct mankind, who " saw the daughters of men that they were fair, and took them wives" [Gen. vi. 2].   For their offence they were " bound in the depths of the earth," and

their giant offspring destroyed. Their " demons,"
however, have the power to corrupt mankind under
the leadership of Mastêmâ, until the judgement and
the establishment of the Messianic kingdom.

It is hardly necessary to point out how closely
this teaching is either allegorically or literally reproduced in the New Testament (see Rev. vii. 1, 2, xiv. 18,
xvi. 5; Matt. xii. 43–5; Luke xi. 24–6; Mark iii. 22;
Matt. viii. 29; Rev xx. 2–3).

The title of the book refers to the peculiar reckoning of chronology employed by the writer—a Sadducæan trait. The forty-nine years of the Jubilee
are divided into seven year-weeks, and events are
dated as occurring on a day of a month in one of
these. The writer includes fifty Jubilees between the
Creation and the entry into Canaan, and, in opposition to the strongly defended Pharisaic reckoning,
adopts the regulations of the year by the solar, not
the lunar, revolutions.

Whether the writer was a Pharisee or a Sadducee,
the book gives us an uncompromising picture of the
heart of Judaism a century before the birth of Christ
We are led into a world where the strongest forces
of traditional piety are used to impress upon a people
tempted to dally with heathen thought and customs
the eternal excellence of their Law. We are in the
atmosphere of those who believe firmly in a righteous,
if also a capricious, God, who, having shown the
path, will most surely judge those who refuse to walk
in it Spiritual presences are present, in man and in
the world, both to tempt and to aid. The Providence
of God is leading, for the Jew is ever optimistic, to
the kingdom of Messiah. And with such religious
certainties are interwoven the fanciful and quaint
ideas with which generations had embroidered the
story of the Patriarchs. We meet also the sterner
and less pleasing side of Jewish conviction—its bondage to the letter, its inhuman stress on the details
of duty, its intense national pride, and utter con-
tempt for the tribes without the Law. In all its fine

qualities and in all its narrow aspects it is the world into which Christ was born. Nay! He speaks the nobler accents of its language : He is bone of its bone and flesh of its flesh. We cannot understand Him, or His struggle with the forces around Him, without understanding this Jewish world. That which He took for His own and baptized with living water for the whole world's use is here, and that which rose against Him, and cried, " We will not have this man to be our King," is here also.

Note —S.P C K edition, by Charles (1917).

THE LETTER OF ARISTEAS

THE writing of pseudonymous epistles was a favourite form of literature in the Roman world. We must not, therefore, be surprised that the Letter of Aristeas, which claims to be the work of a courtier of Ptolemy Philadelphus (285–247 B.C.) and to give an account of contemporaneous events, turns out upon examination to belong to a later date. It contains several statements which make so early a date as the reign of the great Ptolemy impossible, but scholars are not yet agreed as to its real date. Schurer would place it 200 B.C., some German critics as late as A.D. 33, while Dr. Andrews follows Wendland in selecting 96–93 B.C., and supposes it underwent some editing by a later hand.

The Jewish motive throughout is far too obvious for it to have been written by a Greek courtier. The writer is evidently a Pharisaic Jew who adopts the Hellenic disguise in order to introduce his defence of his own religion and nation more easily into Gentile hands. It has been compared to a modern historical novel written with a purpose. This purpose was partly political and partly religious. The sections which deal with the generous action of Ptolemy in releasing his father's Jewish prisoners were no doubt written with a political object, while the description of the translation of the Scriptures by the seventy-two, and the account of the Holy Land, Jerusalem, and the Temple and its services, together with the seventy-two questions solved by the translators, are meant to exalt the Jewish religion, and are fine instances of the constant characteristics of the race. It should be remembered that the translation of the Hebrew Scriptures into Greek was a real landmark, and afforded an unparalleled opportunity amid the decay of religions for Jewish proselytism.

The letter is dedicated to Philocrates, the writer's brother : " My brother in character no less than in blood, but one with me as well in the pursuit of goodness," and begins by telling how Demetrius of Phalerum, the president of the King's library, lamented to the King that among the 200,000 volumes under his charge there was no translation of the Sacred Scriptures of the Jews. Ptolemy determined to remedy the deficiency, and selected Aristeas to go on an embassy to Jerusalem to request the High Priest Eleazar to send a body of scholars to translate the Scriptures at Alexandria. Aristeas thinks this an excellent opportunity to press the King to emancipate the large number of Jews who had been transported from Palestine by his father, some 30,000 of whom were acting as garrisons of the country districts. He suggests that this will be a *quid pro quo* for the privilege, hitherto granted to none, of having the Hebrew Scriptures translated into his own tongue. The King agrees to emancipate the captives, and pays their owners twenty drachmæ a head, the total amount being no less a sum than 660 talents.

In the copy of the decree which is inserted, and which should ever guide the policy of conquerors, Ptolemy says—

" We think that it was against our father's will and against all propriety that they should have been made captives. The spoil which fell to the soldiers on the field of battle was all the booty they should have claimed. To reduce the people to slavery in addition was an act of absolute injustice."

The King sends a gift of 100 talents of silver to Eleazar for the Temple sacrifices, and devotes fifty talents of gold, and seventy of silver, and a wealth of precious stones to the fashioning of fifty libation cups, five bowls, and a magnificent table for the offerings in the Temple, the making of which he personally superintended. This wonderful table with its "mæander" of rubies, emeralds, and onyx, its immense ruby pedestal, and its feet carved like lilies supporting the top, is elaborately described, and gives one no doubt a correct impression of the luxury and artistry of the time. Eleazar grants the King's request, "unusual as it is," and selects six members from each tribe to accompany Aristeas to Alexandria.

A most interesting account of the Temple, city, and country is here interposed, reproduced, it is thought, from a lost work of Hecatæus, and is followed by a disquisition on the enactments of the laws that deal with food, justifying them on allegorical grounds in the manner usual among Alexandrian Jews.

The elders are received with all ceremony by the King, and entertained magnificently for seven days before they begin their labours, the King seating himself with them each night at the banquet. An opportunity is thus given for a display of the gnomic wisdom of the East, Ptolemy nightly propounding twelve questions or problems, which are answered in turn by the elders from Jerusalem.

At the end of the week they are installed in a house on the Pharos Island, where they work daily till three o'clock "in a place which was delightful for its quiet and its brightness," and complete their translation in seventy-two days. It is then read in the presence of the Jewish population, declared to be quite accurate, and a curse is pronounced against any who should tamper with it. Ptolemy receives the scrolls with great satisfaction, and dismisses the translators laden with costly presents.

Such is the account of the origin of the Septuagint, accepted by Josephus, legendary, of course, but free from the marvellous additions of later writers. The whole story is most cleverly contrived to throw every possible ray of glory on the Law and the race that possessed it, and it must have been a useful instrument for Jewish propaganda.

The description of the Temple with its high walls, inexhaustible supply of water, and wonderful cisterns is no doubt accurate : " They led me more than four furlongs outside the city and bade me peer down towards a certain spot and listen to the noise that was made by the meeting of the waters, so that the great size of the reservoirs became manifest to me."

We are shown the orderly and reverent ministration of the 700 priests, each with his own task, to bring wood, or oil, or fine wheat flour, or spices. Some with brawny arms bring the flesh for the burnt-offering, throwing the limbs of a calf weighing more than two talents " with each hand in a wonderful way on to the high place of the altar, and never miss placing them on the proper spot." Others rest hardby till their turn comes, and the place is so still that you would think no human being was present. Then we are told of the majestic Eleazar with his golden bells and variegated pomegranates, his coloured girdle, and the oracle on his breast inscribed with the tribal names, each precious stone " flashing forth in a wondrous way its own particular colour ": his tiara with the sacred names in sacred letters on a plate of gold. " He created such awe and confusion of mind as to make one feel one had come into the presence of a being from another world."

We ascend the citadel that frowns above the Temple with its towers and strong fortifications, its warlike engines and machines, and its 500 guardsmen, who are only allowed to leave their post on feast-days in detachments, and from thence look down upon the city, with its terraced roads, on which the temple-worshippers pass up and down. Their land is of small area, but the Jews are described as an agricultural people cultivating abundant crops, and pasturing great herds of cattle. " The land is thickly planted with multitudes of olive-trees, with crops of corn and pulse, with vines too, and there is

abundance of honey " The country is a commercial
one as well : it handles the gold and precious stones
and spices brought in by the Arabs; it has con-
venient harbours at Askalon, Gaza, Joppa, and
Ptolemais; the Jordan is useful for irrigation; and
it owes much to the natural defences of its narrow
passes, overhanging rocks, and deep ravines. Such
is the smiling picture of Palestine given by this writer
of the first century before Christ.

The disquisition on the Law put into the mouth
of Eleazar paints it as " an impregnable rampart and
wall of iron, that we might not mingle at all with
any of the other nations, but remain pure in body
and soul, free from all vain imaginations, worshipping
the one Almighty God above the whole creation "
Its disciplinary ordinances are all directed to impress
virtue and righteousness on the heart of Israel.
Thus the clean animals in their habits present an
image of peace and holiness, while the unclean are
symbolic of a wild and tyrannous character. " The
division of the hoof " and " the separation of the
claws " remind us of man's duty and privilege to
discriminate between evil and good in every action,
and to abhor the promiscuous sexual intercourse of
the Gentiles. " The chewing of the cud " is a
parable of man's gift of memory, the power he can
exercise of remembering the Divine Presence and
energy morning, noon and night The symbols on
the garments and on the door-posts of the Jew are
likewise, as it were, God's expedient to keep His
people mindful of Him. Above all, the sacrifices
always of tame animals and never of wild, had its
own deep symbolism, " for," said Eleazar, " he who
offers a sacrifice makes an offering also of his own
soul in all its moods."

One can realize how eagerly the nobler souls of
heathenism must have turned from their polluted
rites and contending philosophies to so pure and
rational a conception of God and Duty.

With regard to the seventy-two gnomic answers

of the elders to Ptolemy, they need scarcely detain us. Their wisdom is that of the Proverbs; the greatness of God and the littleness of man is their keynote, and one seems to know the answer before the question is ended. Thus when the King asked, " What is the highest form of glory? " the answer was, " To honour God, and this is not done with gifts and sacrifices, but with purity of soul and holy conviction, since all things are governed and fashioned by God in accordance with His will; of this purpose you are in constant possession, as all men can see from your achievements in the past and in the present."

Some of the answers are of a domestic character; thus the way for a husband to live amicably with his wife is " by recognizing that women are by nature headstrong, and energetic in the pursuit of their own desires, and subject to sudden changes of opinion through fallacious reasoning, and their nature is essentially weak."

The object of this part of the letter is, of course, to magnify the intellectual power and moral insight of the Jews. Thus heathen readers were prepared by Aristeas for the study of the Old Testament Scriptures by a picture of the extravagant generosity that Ptolemy showed the descendants of the patriarchs, by an attractive account of their outward worship, by a panegyric of the purity and truth of their teaching, and by an elaborate exhibition of their intellectual readiness and moral discernment.

Note.—S.P.C K. edition, by Thackeray (1917).

THE BOOKS OF ADAM AND EVE

THE Greek "Apocalypse of Moses" embodied a
mass of legend relating to Adam after the expulsion
from Paradise. It was translated with the addition
of further legendary matter into the Latin "Life of
Adam and Eve." With Christian interpolations it
was translated into many languages, and, united
with the story of the Holy Rood, was a popular book
both in East and West in the fourteenth and fifteenth
centuries. The original work was certainly Jewish,
the Christian additions being obvious patches.

It is always difficult to date a work that contains
no allusions to historical events. The best authorities
are hesitating. Prof. Host thought it might have
been written any time during the first three Christian
centuries. Mr. L. S. A. Wells places it between
A.D. 60 and 300, and as it contains no anti-Christian
polemic considers it was more probably written in
the earlier years of that period by a Jew of the
Dispersion. The Latin "Life" would not be much
later.

The "Apocalypse" begins with Eve's dream about
the death of Abel, but the "Life" tells first of the
penance of Adam and Eve, standing up to their
necks in the water of Jordan. It has the quaint
fancy that the swimming creatures at Adam's invita-
tion came and mourned with him. Satan then comes
and persuades Eve to leave the water, and in answer
to her rebuke recounts the story of his fall, how his
rebellion had followed God's command that the
angels should worship His new-made creature man:
"Worship the image of God as the Lord God hath
commanded." Eve bears Cain, her birth-pangs being

63

assuaged by two angels and two virtues, and "at once the babe ran, and bore a blade of grass in his hand, and took it to his mother."

Then the "Apocalypse" begins, and tells of Eve's dream and of the murder of Abel, and the birth of Seth and Adam's thirty sons and thirty daughters. The account of Adam's vision here follows in the "Life," which is a prophetic and apocalyptic passage, with Christian additions. And last comes the pathetic scene of the death of Adam · he recounts to Seth as he lies in pain how the Lord had said, "Since thou hast abandoned My covenant I have brought upon the body seventy-two strokes; the trouble of the first stroke is a pain of the eyes, the second stroke an affection of the hearing . . ." He sends Eve and Seth towards Paradise to bring him "of the tree out of which the oil floweth," and on the way Seth is assailed by the serpent Outside Paradise the Angel Michael tells them that in no wise can the oil be given till the last days, and that Adam must die in six days. So they go back bearing herbs of fragrance, nard, crocus, calamus, and cinnamon. When they reach home Adam bids them call all his children and grand-children together that Eve may tell them the story of their fall. In her account she tells how the devil poured on the forbidden fruit "the poison of his wickedness, which is lust, the root and beginning of every sin," and how Adam departed from Paradise bearing fragrant herbs for incense to offer to God, and seed to sow for his food.

And Eve said, "How is it that thou diest, and I live, or how long have I to live after thou art dead? Tell me!" And Adam saith, "Reck not of this, for thou tarriest not after me, but even both of us are to die together. And you shall be laid in my place. But when I die anoint me, and let no man touch me till the angel of the Lord shall speak somewhat concerning me. For God will not forget me, but will seek His own creature."

When Adam dies Eve sees him borne away by the chariot of the Seraphim, and the angels praying for his pardon, and at length he is borne to rest in the third heaven. His body is transferred to Paradise by the Lord Himself together with that of Abel, and prepared for burial. He is buried in the place where God found the dust. "And God called and said, 'Adam, Adam.' And the body answered from the grave and said, 'Here am I, Lord.' And God saith to him : 'I told thee that earth thou art, and to earth shalt thou return. Again I promise thee the Resurrection. I will raise thee up in the Resurrection, with every man who is of thy seed."

In six days Eve also dies, but before death she prays to be buried with Adam : "Just as in our transgression we were both led astray and transgressed Thy command but were not separated—even so, Lord, do not separate us now." So the angels came and buried her with Adam and Abel

The most striking thing in these legends is the extremely crude and anthropomorphic ideas of God. It goes far beyond the primitive records of Genesis, and shows what the Jewish public appreciated, in spite of the elaborate spiritualizing of Old Testament conceptions that had gone on in Alexandria.

The teaching about the Future Life, the Resurrection, the Judgement, and the state of departed souls in the third heaven is that of later Judaism

The book is full of the poetry that the dying figure of Adam cannot fail to evoke, and there are many sayings in it about death and life which by their *naïve* simplicity touch the roots of human feeling. It is from this book that Mr. Binyon has drawn the materials for his striking poem, "The Death of Adam."

Note —The Book is most accessible in Charles, *Apocrypha and Pseudepigrapha*, Vol. II. (Wells).

E

THE MARTYRDOM OF ISAIAH

THE Martyrdom of Isaiah is combined with the
Vision of Isaiah and the Testament of Hezekiah to
form the Ascension of Isaiah, which were the work
of Christian writers. But the Martyrdom is by a
Jew, who agrees in his account with the Talmud,
which states that a document was found in Jerusalem
describing Isaiah's death   Of this Jewish record the
Martyrdom is probably a Greek translation; as
it seems to be quoted in the Epistle to the Hebrews
(xi 37), it is probably a first-century document.

It tells how Hezekiah calls Manasseh, his son, and
Isaiah, and gives them his last command (i. 1-2).
The prophet foretells Manasseh's apostasy and his
own martyrdom, which nothing that Hezekiah can
do can prevent (i. 6-13). Hezekiah dies, and
Manasseh gives himself up to all kinds of sin (ii. 1-7).
Isaiah departs to Bethlehem, and then to the mountains, where he stays two years with the prophets
fasting and lamenting (ii 10-16)   Belchira, a false
prophet discovers him, and accuses him to Manasseh,
on the grounds that he had professed to see God, and
had called Jerusalem Sodom, and its princes and
people Gomorrah (iii. 1-12)   Isaiah is sawn asunder
(v. 1-14).

The " wooden saw " of the Greek is a misunder-
standing of the Hebrew original, which must have been
" a saw for sawing wood."

Dr. Charles connects the story with a Persian legend
of King Djemchid, for whom God caused a tree to
open to conceal him from his rival; by the help of

66

Iblis he is discovered, and the tree is sawn asunder with Djemchid inside it.

The story has its basis no doubt in 2 Kings xxi 16, and is an example of a Jewish *Midrash*

An attempt has been made by M. Halévy (*Etudes evangeliques*, I. pp. 65 ff) to find in it a source of the story of our Lord's Temptation   The idea is very properly dismissed by Canon Box in his edition in this series as far-fetched   The account of Isaiah's temptation is " remote both in substance and in spirit from the sublime narrative in the Gospels " Canon Box finds interesting light on the Jewish demonology of the period in the book   Thus we have Beliar (= Belial) as a name of the Prince of evil spirits.   He is " the Angel of lawlessness, who is the ruler of this world " (cf John xii 31, xvi, 11, 2 Cor iv. 4, Eph vi 12)   Sammael also appears, the " Venom of God," here represented as " chief of the Satans " (cf Matt. ix 34)   He is regarded by Canon Charles as the subordinate of Beliar, executing his orders.   Belial also has the mysterious name of Matanbûchûs, which Halévy thinks expresses the power of the demon " to take possession " (Hebrew MITHDABEK).

The designation of the Messiah as " The Beloved " is also a characteristic of the book, though it remains undecided whether it was in the Jewish version before it was included in the Ascension of Isaiah.

Note —S P.C K. edition.   Translation, Charles, Introduction, Box.

THE ETHIOPIC BOOK OF ENOCH

The Book of Enoch is by far the most important of the apocalyptic works after Daniel. It is in reality a collection of writings of various dates during the first two centuries B C It reflects a great variety of religious ideas not always in harmony with one another, bound together by a unity of tone and outlook, while subject to the development of free intellectual movement Its earliest portions come from the "pious" predecessors of the Pharisees, while throughout it is representative of the Pharisaic school. By the "pious" Jews, or *Chasidim*, are meant the conservative minority of the pre-Maccabæan age, who refused in any way to absorb Hellenistic culture. In their simple faithfulness to the Law they were opposed to the governing classes In post-Maccabæan days they became the ancestors both of the Pharisees and of the apocalyptic writers. The Pharisees represented in an exaggerated form their strict adherence to the Law, the Apocalyptists stood for their simple and specifically Jewish faith.[1]

Though almost unknown in the Western Church until recent times, no pseudepigraphic book had a higher place in the Jewish Church of our Lord's day, or a deeper or more extensive influence on the writers of the New Testament. Its return to recognition is due to the great traveller Bruce, who brought back from Abyssinia in 1773 the three MSS. in Ethiopic, from which Lawrence made the first modern translation.

Enoch contains fragments of an older work, the Book of Noah, of whose existence we have independent

[1] See Oesterley, *The Books of the Apocrypha*, p. 93 (quoting Friedländer, *Die rel Bewegungen*, p. 22).

evidence in the Book of Jubilees. Canon Charles gives the Noah portions scattered through Enoch as chapters vi.-xi., liv.-lv. 2, lx., lxv.-lxix. 25, and cvi. and cvii.

The book was arranged by its last editor in five sections, like the Psalms and other Jewish Books.

Section I. (i -xxxvi). This mainly recounts Enoch's pronouncing of God's judgement on the Watchers, the angels who fell through their love for the daughters of men (Gen vi. 1-4), and his intercession for them It contains lurid and weird descriptions of the world of Hades

Section II. (xxxvii -lxxi.)   This contains three " Parables," or apocalyptic revelations, and the account of Enoch's translation

Section III (lxxii -lxxxii). This is in reality in the main a treatise on astronomy, dealing with the unchanging order of the heavenly bodies.

Section IV. (lxxxiii -xc). Enoch recounts to Methuselah his Visions of the Deluge, the Fall of the Angels, and their punishment in the underworld, the deliverance of Noah, the Exodus, the giving of the Law, and the occupation of Palestine, the time of the Judges, the Kingship and the Building of the Temple, and the story of the two Kingdoms to the Fall of Jerusalem. Then come the four periods of angelic rule up to the Maccabæan Revolt, the last assault of the Gentiles, and the Judgement.   And last, the foundation of the New Jerusalem, the Conversion of the Gentiles, the Resurrection of the Righteous, and the Advent of the Messiah " the hornèd Lamb, over whom the Lord of the sheep rejoiced "

Section V (xci.-civ)   This is a book of warning containing the denunciation of woes on sinners, and the promise of blessings on the righteous. It contains an older work, " The Apocalypse of Weeks " (xciii. 1-10, xci. 12-19). It concludes (cv.) · " In those days the Lord bade to summon and testify to the children of earth concerning their wisdom : show (it) unto them ; for ye are their guides, and a

recompense over the whole earth. For I and My
Son will be united with them for ever in the paths
of uprightness in their lives; and ye shall have
peace; rejoice, ye children of uprightness. Amen."

With regard to the dates of the various sections,
Canon Charles gives—

Book of Noah, not later than 161 B.C.
Section I , not later than 170 B C.
Section II., either 94–79 or 70–64 B.C.
Section III., not later than 110 B C.
Section IV , not later than 161 B C.
Section V., during oppression of Pharisees, either
95–79 or 70–64 B.C.

With regard to the relation of the Enoch literature
to the New Testament, (1) while in Section I we have
gross and materialistic ideas of the future life, in
Section V. we find the spiritual ideas of our Lord
expressed in Matt xxii 30.

(11) While in chapter xc. a human Messiah is suggested as head of the Messianic nation, in Section II.
we have a Messiah portrayed, who has the four titles
of " Christ," or the Anointed One, the " Righteous
One," the " Elect One," and the " Son of Man," which
are reproduced in the New Testament. For the
first time " Christ " becomes the title of the future
ideal Ruler, and the definite title " Son of Man " " is
found for the first time in Jewish literature, and is,
historically, the source of the New Testament designation, and contributes to it some of its characteristic
contents " (Charles).

(111) In Enoch we pass from the Old Testament
doctrine of the world after death to something more
in accord with the New. " The Resurrection," says
Canon Charles, " was made a commonplace of Jewish
theology by 1 Enoch "

(1v) The demonic background of the New Testament assumed in the reported teaching of Jesus is
essentially the demonology of Enoch. The demons
are disembodied spirits awaiting their final punishment, subject to Satan, who is head of a kingdom of

evil, leads men and angels astray, and whose functions
are tempting, accusing, and punishing (1 Cor. v. 5).
See Matt. viii. 29, xii. 24–28; Matt. iv. 1–12; 2 Cor.
xi. 3; Rev. xii. 4 and 10

The following are typical examples of the reproduction of the actual phraseology of Enoch in the
New Testament:

Matt. xix. 28. When
the Son of Man shall sit
on the throne of his
glory.
Ye also shall sit on
twelve thrones.

lxii. 5. When they see
that Son of Man [i.e. the
Messiah] sitting on the
throne of his glory.
cviii. 12. I will seat
each on the throne of
honour.

xix. 29 Inherit eternal
life.

xl. 9. Inherit eternal
life.

xxvi. 24 It had been
good for that man if he
had not been born.

xxxviii. 2. It had been
good for them, if they
had not been born.

John v. 22. He hath
committed all judgement
unto the Son.

lxix. 27. The sum of
judgement was given unto
the Son of Man.

Acts iv. 12. None other
name . . . whereby we
must be saved.
1 Cor. vi. 11. Justified
in the name of the Lord
Jesus.

xlviii. 7. In His [i e.
the Messiah's] name they
are saved.

Rom. viii. 38. Angels
. . . principalities. . .
powers.

lxi 10. Angels of power
. . . and angels of prin-
cipalities.

Col. ii. 3 In whom are
hid all the treasures of
wisdom and knowledge.

xlvi. 3 The Son of
Man . . . who reveals all
the treasures of that
which is hidden.

Rev. iii. 20. I will come
in to him, and will sup
with him, and he with
me.

lxii 14 And with that
Son of Man shall they [i e
the righteous] eat and lie
down and rise up

The book of Revelation is especially full of reminiscences of Enoch : *e. g.*

> The tree of life, ii. 7.
> The white raiment, iii. 5.
> The angels of the winds, vii. 1.
> The star falling from heaven, ix. 1.
> The lake of fire, xx. 15.

Note.—S P C.K edition, by Charles.

THE TESTAMENTS OF THE TWELVE PATRIARCHS

In the Library of Cambridge University is the MS of the Testaments of the Twelve Patriarchs obtained in the thirteenth century by the famous English scholar, Robert Grosseteste, the saintly Bishop of Lincoln. He in his simplicity believed with the men of his day that it contained actually the last words of the twelve sons of Jacob   Scholars of our own time are less simple, and have little difficulty in ascertaining the approximate date of its first appearance; they know that its ascription to the Twelve Patriarchs is but one instance of the custom of apocalyptic writers · they look for information in it about the thought of the age in which it really was produced, and are richly rewarded. This was the time of John Hyrcanus, the very zenith of Maccabæan glory, who at the moment was regarded because of his holding the offices of prophet, priest, and king, and for his military successes, as the actual fulfilment of the hopes of a Messiah.   As such he was the idol of the Pharisaic party up to the year 106 B C , when the deadly breach occurred, which separated him from them. The original book was perhaps written in Hebrew by a Pharisaic admirer who did not scruple to include in his works psalms to his idol of a Messianic character, at any rate before the breach occurred   Interwoven with this original work are later passages that paint the later Hasmonæan rule in the most hostile colours. The dynasty had become corrupt, and the Pharisaic spirit, unchanging in its hopes for the future of Israel, now turned with loathing from the family that had once loomed so large.   And thus we have curses of the Hasmonæans intermingled with blessings on their

great predecessor John Hyrcanus. Having been content for a time to waive their conviction that the
Messiah would spring from the tribe of Judah, when
events taught them their mistake, they returned all
the more eagerly to their ancient hope.

Canon Charles regards the chief interest of the work
to be its high and spiritual ethical teaching, " which,"
he says, " has achieved a real immortality by influenc-
ing the thought and diction of the writers of the New
Testament, and even those of our Lord."

Besides the Jewish additions, which were made
somewhere about B.C. 60, we find a number of Christian interpolations of a dogmatic character, which
are easily detected. For the book was very popular
with the early Church.

Theories have been advanced by some English
scholars that all resemblances between the New
Testament and the Testaments are due to an editor who
transferred matter from the former to the latter
Canon Charles pronounces emphatically against this
view. The merely dogmatic interpolations are obvious from their disagreement with the teaching of the
book as a whole : " the ethical sayings and teachings
are in harmony not only with the spirit of the book
as a whole, but also with their respective contexts." [1]
So that these theories may be definitely dismissed.

The method of the writer is to give one by one an
imaginary speech from the lips of each dying patriarch, they are partly ethical, partly apocalyptic ; the
ethical teaching springs from the character of the
patriarch himself in each case as painted in Genesis
or later legend ; thus Reuben deals from his own
supposed experience with the fire of lust, Simeon with
the canker of envy, and Levi exalts the beauty of
holiness. The ethical teaching, therefore, is winged
with a certain dramatic force, unknown to the more
prosaic Wisdom-writers And then as he looks far
down the vista of the future and sees the events of
later ages hurrying on to crisis, or established in

[1] *Apocrypha and Pseudepigrapha, O.T* , II p 291.

peace, he seems to burst forth naturally into the great apocalyptic passages, as exalted as any that are preserved, in their assurance of the supernatural righteousness and glory of the Messianic Kingdom, which shall include all nations.

As has been said, the book exerted a strong influence on the New Testament. Canon Charles notes that St. Paul used it as a *vade mecum*, and finds some seventy words in St Paul's Epistles, common to the Testaments, which are not found elsewhere in the New Testament. The rather-strange expression in Rom. i. 32 is really a reproduction of an expression in the Testament of Asher vi 2. With regard to our Lord's teaching we find in Test. Gad. vi. 3 (β) : *If any one sin against thee speak to him in peace . . . and if he repent forgive him* (cf Matt. xviii. 15)

And the Test Dan. v. 3 conjoins like Jesus the two chief duties : " Love the Lord in all your life, and one another with a true heart " (cf Matt xxii 37-39) Several cases of identity of expression are to be found.

The author of the Testaments, unlike other Pharisees of his day with whose works we are acquainted, as well as the later interpolator, is a Universalist. He believes that the Gentile world will be saved through Israel. This conviction alone marks the spiritual development that his faith had reached His doctrine of the Messiah is coloured by the fact that he believed him to spring from the priestly tribe. He is the Mediator, who opens Paradise to the righteous, gives them to eat of the tree of life, binds the spirit of evil, and destroys the reign of sin. As prophet he teaches the holy nation, and as king he rules and destroys its enemies. In the Resurrection, after the rising of the patriarchs and heroes, the righteous will stand on the right hand and the wicked on the left The New Jerusalem will be founded on earth, and will last for ever

Note —S.P C K edition, by Charles.

THE SIBYLLINE ORACLES

THE story of the Cumæan Sibyl, who brought her books of oracles to Tarquin, is a commonplace of Roman History. It was the accepted explanation in the time of Livy of the fact that certain oracular rolls were laid up in the Capitol from the days of the founding of the Roman state, to be referred to for guidance in the hour of national stress. These books play their part in the religion of Rome until their destruction by fire in 82 B.C. ; they were then replaced by a selection of similar oracles collected from Sicily, Greece, and Asia Minor.

The earliest and most famous of these oracular Sibyls was the Erythræan, but in course of time many were recognized as showing this peculiar form of inspiration. The early Fathers, Clement of Rome, Justin Martyr, and Clement of Alexandria, quote from them, while Augustine does not hesitate to admit them to the City of God (De Civ Dei. xviii. 23). There was then a considerable quantity of Sibyllic prophecy in circulation in antiquity in addition to that officially recognized as concerned with the destinies of Rome. Some of it was venerable with age, some of it appeared in response to the needs of the time, novel and fresh. It lay in the archives of private families, it became incorporated in histories, it ran rapidly in its easily remembered hexameters from mouth to mouth, and from land to land   It was a real expression of the sense of divine purpose, the certainty of judgement, the capriciousness of fate, as men felt themselves to be involved in the bewildering stress of events.

We have to ask what the relation of our so-called

Sibylline Books was to this mass of mostly perished literature. These books, originally fifteen in number, now comprise twelve, and consist of over four thousand lines   What is the decision of scholars as to their connection with the heathen utterances ?
The answer is that " they are a compilation of old and new oracles worked up by Jewish and Christian authors who lived at various times between 160 B C. and the fifth century, or even later, A.D " (Lanchester in Charles's *Apoc and Pseudepig.* ii 368). It is with the Jewish portion that we have to do here, or rather with the portion that is not decidedly Christian, for we are on very debateable ground. This consists of two fragments, and three books, III , IV., and V.   Book III is probably the work of an Egyptian Jew living about 140 B C.   There is little doubt that he has incorporated large sections of Sibylline work. Notably there is a piece of 700 lines, which may have been the poem of the Erythræan Sibyl, alluded to by Lactantius (*Div Inst* i. 6).   It tells the story of the Titans and the birth of Zeus, in the manner of Hesiod, and of the building of Babylon, and gives a short summary of Jewish history.   The original poem was probably written about 160 B.C. as it refers to Ptolemy Philometer.   The whole book has references to the desecration of the Temple by Antiochus 168 B.C. and his attack on Egypt 170 B.C.   It refers to the prosperity of the days of Simon 140 B C   It seems to refer in Roman history to the Mithridatic, Social, Punic and Greek wars of 88, 89, and 146 B.C.
There is a long section pronouncing woes on heathen lands, especially Greece, and eschatological passages which describe the coming of the Messiah, and the signs of the end.
Book IV., after promising a history of the ten generations of the world, turns after the second to denunciation of the wickedness of heathen countries and towns.   It contains an eschatological passage, and speaks of the restoration of Laodicea after the earthquake of 60 A.D., the siege of Jerusalem and

the destruction of the Temple, the disappearance of Nero and the strange expectation of his return, and the earthquake in Cyprus of A.D. 76.

Book V, if we neglect the statements of three lines, which seem to be interpolated, seems to have been written in the earlier years of Hadrian, *circa* A D. 130. It gives a short sketch of history up to Hadrian, and denounces doom on the nations one by one. It includes also a poem on " Pride," a description of Judæa, a striking eschatological passage, and a prophecy of the battle of the stars. There is here, as in the earlier books, much of the local colouring of Egypt, whence the book must have emanated.

The contents of this strange *mélange* of the Western and the Eastern spirits shows clearly enough the motive of their production. To Jew and Christian alike the manner and matter of these widely spread writings appealed as a useful instrument to popularize the truth. So far as these scattered leaves were inspired by the Spirit of God they could, though not written by the children of the Covenant, be pressed into the service of the propaganda of the true faith. The awe that clung around them in the popular mind, and the fulfilment, evident to the trustful, of many of their predictions, procured a respectful hearing for the word of life couched in their ancient form. The Jewish adapter knew nothing of copy-right, and coveted no literary fame. He was zealous to proselytize, and to deliver the world that lay in wickedness from its bondage to the flesh and the devil. And with this high aim we see him pouring the ideals of Jewish prophecy through a heathen instrument, and making the venerable figure of the Sibyl the exponent of the Law of Jehovah. If we shrink from the lack of honesty in his methods, it is because we are transferring the literary code of morals in our own time to his. We should at least admire the recognition of the unity of inspiration, revealed to the Jewish thinker in the outpourings of the heathen prophetess and in his own sacred seers.

To give a general idea of the spirit of the Sibyllines let us take a few typical passages showing the attitude of the writer to the idolatry of the heathen world, to the doctrine of the true God, and to the coming judgement and Messianic Kingdom.

Thus he writes of God:

> " There is one sovereign God, ineffable, whose dwelling is in Heaven, self-sprung, unseen yet seeing all himself alone   No mason's hand did make him, nor does some model formed from gold or ivory by the varied skill of man represent him.   But he, himself, Eternal, hath revealed himself as One who is, and was before, and shall be hereafter . . . Ye do not worship nor fear God, but wander at haphazard, bowing down to serpents, and doing sacrifice to cats, and to dumb idols and stone statues of mortals, and sitting down before the doors of godless temples, ye weary the God who ever is, who guards all, taking your delight in miserable stones, forgetting the judgement of the Eternal Saviour, Who created heaven and earth."   (III. 11–35)

And of Rome ·

> " O Rome, pampered golden offspring of Latium !   Thou virgin intoxicated by thy many suitors in marriage, as a slave-girl shalt thou be wedded without ceremony, and ofttimes shall thy mistress shear thy luxuriant locks, and passing sentence on thee shall cast thee from heaven to earth, and shall lift thee up again from earth to heaven, because men held to a bad and shameless life."   (III. 356–361)

He cries to Greece :

> " Hellas, why dost thou put thy trust in governors, mortal men who are powerless to

escape the consummation of death? With what
view dost thou offer vain gifts to the dead, and
sacrifice to idols? Who has put error in thy
heart, that thou shouldst perform these rites and
forsake the face of Mighty God?" (III. 545–549)

And in his panegyric on his own countrymen he
sings of a

" holy race of God-fearing men, adhering to the
counsel and the mind of the Most High; who
pay full honour to the temple of the Mighty God
with drink-offerings and fat-offerings and sacred
hecatombs, with sacrifices of lusty bulls and un-
blemished rams, and piously offer as whole burnt
sacrifices rich flocks of firstling sheep and lambs
upon the great altar. . . . They raise to heaven
holy hands, rising early from their bed, and ever
cleansing their flesh with water, and honour him
alone who reigns for ever the Eternal, and after
him their parents : and more than any men
they are mindful of the purity of marriage."
(III. 573–595)

And these verses come from the description of the
Messianic age.

" And then from the sunrise God shall send
a King, who shall give every land relief from the
bane of war; some he shall slay and to others he
shall consecrate faithful vows. Nor shall he
do these things by his own will, but in obedience
to the good ordinances of the Mighty God. . . .
From heaven shall fall fiery swords down to the
earth; lights shall come bright and great, flashing
into the midst of men. . . . And God shall
judge all with war and sword, and with fire and
cataclysms of rain. . . . Then again all the sons
of the great God shall live quietly around the
temple, rejoicing in those gifts which He shall

give who is the Creator and sovereign righteous
Judge. For he by himself shall shield them
standing beside them alone in his might, encir-
cling them as it were with a well of flaming fire. . .
And then all the isles and the cities shall say,
How doth the Eternal love those men ! For all
things work in sympathy with them and help
them, the heaven and God's chariot, the Sun,
and the Moon " (III. 652–712.)

The allusion to Homer as having stolen the Sibyl's
measure is famous:

" Then again there shall be an aged man
false in writing, and false in birthplace; and the
light in his eyes shall set Yet he shall have
much wit and a verse fitted to his thoughts
blended under two names. Chian shall he call
himself and he shall write the story of Ilium,
not truthfully indeed but with poetic skill, for
he shall gain possession of my verses and mea-
sures. He first shall unfold my books with his
hand, and then right well shall he deck out the
armed men of war, Hector, Priam's son, and
Achilles, born of Peleus, and all the rest who
care for doughty deeds. Yea, and he shall
make gods stand by the heroes' side, leading
astray in every way the mortals of empty head.
Their widespread glory will it be to have died
in Ilium, but he himself shall receive his recompense." (III. 319–331.)

Note.—S.P C K. edition, by Bate (1918).

F

THE ASSUMPTION OF MOSES

THE fragment known by this name exists in only one MS., which was discovered at Milan and published in 1864. It probably dates from the sixth century A D. It does not contain any account of the Assumption, and seems to exclude the teaching that Moses was taken up into heaven, and therefore the fragment we have is hardly likely to be even a part of the book from which St. Jude quotes. Our book is rather a " Testament," or farewell-speech, similar to the Testaments of the Twelve Patriarchs. It is supposed by Canon Charles, however, that in it we have one portion of a composite work that was known as " The Assumption," and that the other portion has perished. Prof. F C. Burkitt holds that the original MS represented a single work, and that the part containing the account of the Assumption has been lost.

From internal evidence there seems every probability that this book was actually written in our Lord's childhood or youth, *i e* between A.D 7 and 30 and its author is a Pharisee of a type fast passing away, a descendant of the ancient " righteous " non-resisting believers in the Law, who while believing in the coming Divine judgement, were content to leave the national future in God's hands, and to make no efforts to work deliverance by violent means. Thus he has no eulogy of the Maccabees, but praises the patient martyr Eleazar who retired with his sons from the evils of the world, and perished in a cave. Canon Charles regards the book as a " direct protest from the inner ring of conservative Pharisaism against the popular secularization of the ideals of the

righteous." These had become " fused with political
ideals and popular Messianic beliefs," and required
to be led back to the conviction that God would
Himself vindicate His purposes. Like our Lord he
foresaw the doom to which his country was hastening,
and warned her, as has been said, " with the unheeded
voice of a Cassandra."

The book describes how Moses at the point of
death delivers the sacred books to Joshua; he prophesies the entry into Canaan, the rule of the judges,
the kingship, and the breaking-away of the ten tribes.
He tells of the corruption of the national religion,
and of the captivity under Nebuchadnezzar   He tells
how one tribe shall say to another: " Lo, is not
this that which Moses did once declare unto us in
prophecies? Yea, he declared and called heaven
and earth to witness against us that we should not
transgress the commandments of the Lord, of which
he was the mediator to us." He gives the prayer of
Daniel, and the return of the two tribes, and the
increase of the ten tribes in captivity. He describes
in strong terms the idolatry of the Priests, and the
progress of Hellenism, and denounces the Maccabees
" Then shall arise over them kings to reign, and they
shall be called Priests of the Most High God, and they
shall work impiety in the Holy of Holies," referring
to the priesthood being made hereditary in the family
of the Maccabees in 141 B C. He tells of the enormities of Herod, the conquest of the Romans, and the
degradation of the leaders of his own day. After
the eulogy of the patient Eleazar, he gives a striking
apocalyptic passage, and the book concludes with the
encouragement of Joshua to undertake with a good
courage the heritage of Moses' work. As a review of
Jewish history it stands out with marked features,
and gives us a particular attitude towards the work of
the Maccabees, which we could hardly have suspected
to have existed in such strength. It is particularly
valuable as showing that among the various parties
around our Lord, there was at least one which was

in sympathy with his national aims, though it was
the very party which apparently disclaimed any hope
of a Messiah.

There are striking similarities in the apocalyptic
passage to our Lord's Prophecy of the last things,
which raise questions of the deepest interest—

" . . . For the Heavenly One shall arise from the
    throne of His Kingdom
And shall come out of His holy habitation
With indignation and wrath for His children.
And the earth shall quake; even to its bounds shall
    it be shaken :
And the lofty mountains shall be brought low and
    shall be shaken.
And the valleys shall fall
The sun shall not give his light, and the horns of
    the moon shall be turned into darkness,
And they shall be broken, and the whole of the
    moon shall be turned into blood
And the circuit of the stars shall be disordered;
And the sea shall fall into the abyss :
The fountains of waters shall fail;
And the rivers be afraid."

(X. 3–7.)

Such passages, which of course are not rare in the
apocalyptic writers, enforce the conclusion that our
Lord in the language of His apocalyptic teaching was
drawing upon a mass of popular and somewhat
stereotyped expression that had been passed on
from age to age, and aroused a vague and vast sense
of coming doom. This consideration relieves us from
looking for the literal fulfilment in detail of such of
His prophecies, as have to do with the physical world.

Note.—S.P.C K edition, by Ferrar (with *Apoc Baruch*).

THE SECRETS OF ENOCH

THE Book of the Secrets of Enoch is a quite distinct work from the Ethiopic Book of Enoch. It was discovered by Canon Charles to be surviving in a Slavonic version, after remaining unknown for twelve centuries. It was written in Egypt by a Hellenistic Jew early in the first century A.D. It must have been an important work in its day, for it is quoted in most of the apocalyptic books of the first century. It was written in Greek, though it seems to incorporate Hebrew portions. And it is largely pervaded by the Greek spirit, embodying the philosophical ideas of Philo, and neglecting the Old Testament view of the Messiah. The author was an enlightened but orthodox Jew, especially in his teaching on sacrifice, and the future life. He allowed himself full liberty to combine in his work views from very different sources—the Platonic, the Egyptian, and the Zend; and was therefore probably an example of the Jewish culture of Alexandria. The book tells how in his three hundred and sixty-fifth year Enoch is taken up by the angels, at God's command, and passes through the ten heavens. In the first heaven Enoch sees the angels who rule the stars, and those who keep the storehouses of the snow and of the dew. In the second are the apostate angels, who beseech him to pray for them. The third heaven is Paradise, " and the tree of life is in the midst of the garden, in the place whereon the Lord rests when He goes up into Paradise . . . Its root is in the garden at the world's end." It is the abode of the just and charitable. The abode of the lost is there as well with its gloom and fiery river,

its snow and ice, its thirst and shivering. Through
the fourth heaven go the courses of the sun and moon.
There are the great gates through which they pass,
and Enoch hears the song of the elements of the sun,
and the wonderful music of the angels, " sweet and
incessant, which it is impossible to describe." In
the fifth heaven he sees the Satans, or " Grigori,"
the original heavenly rebels, sad and silent, who at
his rebuke break into a pitiful song to the Lord. In
the sixth are the archangels and the angels of Nature
singing at God's footstool, while the seventh is the
precinct of God's throne; there the angelic orders come
in turn to the steps and " sing songs in the boundless
light with small and tender voices." It is in the tenth
Heaven that Enoch is brought into the Presence, and
sees God's face. There he is anointed and robed in
glorious garments, and writes the three hundred and
sixty-five books of all knowledge, and of all human
destiny, and sitting by Gabriel hears the great secrets
of God, how He formed the visible from the invisible:
" for before all things were visible, I alone used to go
about in the invisible things, like sun from east to
west, and from west to east. But even the sun has
peace in itself, while I found no peace——" : how
heaven and the angels, and earth were formed—and
lastly man " of seven consistencies, his flesh from the
earth, his blood from the dew, his eyes from the sun,
his bones from stone, his intelligence from the swift-
ness of the angels and from cloud; his veins and hair
from the grass of the earth; his soul from My breath
and from wind." Man is child both of visible and
invisible, he is a second angel, and bears the name
ADAM, whose four letters are the initials of the four
quarters. Enoch is told to hand on the books to
his children, and to return to earth to teach them for
thirty days. The rest of the book contains his instruction. He inculcates obedience to rulers, a life of
kindness and charity, and altogether deprecates the
value of sacrifice: "God demands pure hearts, and
with all that only tests the heart of man." Swearing

is forbidden: "If there is no truth in men let them swear by the words 'yea, yea,' or else 'nay, nay.'" And they are to return good for evil. It is striking to find kindness to animals dwelt upon; in fact the souls of the animals "will not perish, till the great judgement, and they will accuse man, if he feed them ill."

All the duties of life are to be done with the pervading sense that it is the world of God's creation in which we are involved, and that God sees everything. "If you look to heaven the Lord is there; if you take thought of the sea's depth, and all the underworld the Lord is there."

The book ends with an account of a three-days' feast after Enoch's final translation.

There are many striking similarities of expression and thought which seem to show that the writers of the New Testament are in some measure dependent on this book. In the Gospels "Blessed are the peacemakers," recalls "Blessed is he who implants peace." The verse (xlix. 1): "I swear not by oath, neither by heaven, nor by earth, nor by any other creature . . . if there is no truth in them let them swear by the words 'yea, yea' or 'nay, nay,'" is surely the basis of Matt. v 34–37. Again, John xiv. 2 is certainly connected with: "In the great time to come—are many mansions prepared for men, good for the good, bad for the bad" (lxi 2). There are also many striking parallels with St. Paul and Hebrews; e. g. xlii. 12: "Blessed is he in whom is truth, that he may speak truth to his neighbour" (cf. Eph. iv. 25), and xxv. 1: "I commanded . . . that visible things should come down from invisible" seems to be at the back of Heb. xi 3 · "What is seen hath not been made of things that do appear." In Revelation there are similar likenesses, e. g. ix. 1: "There was given to him the key of the pit of the abyss," cf. "The keyholders and guards of the gates of hell" (xlii. 1).

Note —Charles and Morfill's edition (1896).

II. BARUCH

THIS interesting book only exists in a Syriac translation from the Greek, which was itself translated from
the Hebrew. It is one of many works attributed to
Baruch. It must have been written after the Fall of
Jerusalem A.D. 70, and probably before the end of
the century. It is, therefore, contemporaneous with
the great mass of New Testament literature, " and
furnishes records of the Jewish doctrines and beliefs
of that period, and of the arguments which prevailed
in Judaism in the latter half of the first century,
with which its leaders sought to uphold its declining
faith and confront the attacks of a growing and
aggressive Christianity" (Charles). It is a last example
from the standpoint of orthodox Pharisaism, of the
freer and more poetical side of Jewish thought, and
though generally pessimistic in tone, has still its
glorious visions of a bright Messianic future.

Scholars differ as to whether it is of composite or
single authorship. To Canon Charles its conflicting
views of the Messiah and other points of theology,
and the interblended light and shade of its outlook
make it certainly composite. Clemen, on the other
hand, holds that the writer merely incorporated vary-
ing apocalyptic matter, while Prof. Burkitt lays stress
on the likelihood that a seer's visions at different
periods faithfully recorded are not bound to be har-
monious. All would agree that it includes an amount
of earlier material, somewhat crudely put together.

The book is supposed to be Baruch's account of
what happened to him at the time of the destruction
of Jerusalem, but, as Dr. Oesterley remarks, " the

narrative is to be understood as referring to the present time from the author's point of view." It falls
into seven sections, of which the following is a short
synopsis.

I. (i.–xii). The imminent fall of the city is an-
nounced, and the Chaldæans come. But four angels
overthrow the walls, and bury the holy things of the
Temple, and a voice is heard : " Enter ye enemies, for
he who kept the house has forsaken it."

II. (xiii.–xx.). The question of the incomprehensible
judgements of God, by which the righteous suffer, is
considered. The counsel is : " Look to the end."
" For now it is the consummation of time that should
be considered, whether of business, or prosperity, or
shame, and not the beginning thereof " (xix 5).

III. (xxi.–xxxiv.). The time of tribulation for the
wicked of the whole earth is foretold, leading up to
the Messianic age. Baruch tells the elders that the
Law is to be their stay, amid the fall of everything
around them.

IV. (xxxv –xlvi). Baruch's vision of the cedar and
the vine, which remains when the cedar is dust.
The cedar is probably Pompey, and the vine is the
Messiah. Baruch is told of his coming death

V. (xlvii.–lii). Account of the Resurrection Body.
For the sake of recognition all will rise exactly as they
lived on earth ; after the judgement the transformation
to glory or shame shall take place.

VI. (liii.–lxxvi) The vision of the cloud rising out
of the sea, the water beneath is alternately dark and
bright twelve times. Thus is portrayed the successive
faithfulness and apostasy of the Jewish people. The
culmination is the appearance of twelve rivers typify-
ing the Messiah's reign.

VII. (lxxvii.–lxxxvii.). Baruch sends two letters :
one to the nine and a half tribes, and the other to the
two and a half tribes in Babylon. The latter is not
given, and is supposed by Canon Charles to be partially
incorporated in the apocryphal Baruch 1. The former
insists that the exiles suffer a just judgement of God,

that their oppressors shall be punished, and that they must observe the Law rigidly.

" The righteous have been gathered,
  And the prophets have fallen asleep;
  And we also have gone forth from the land,
  And Zion has been taken from us ;
  And we have nothing now save the
  Mighty One and His Law." (LXXXV. 3.)

Baruch binds the letter to the neck of the eagle, who is to carry it, and the book ends somewhat abruptly.

The teaching of the book elucidates that of our Lord and of St. Paul by contrast. We see how an orthodox Pharisee felt about the paramount duty of obedience both to the oral and the written Law. " Shepherds, and lamps, and fountains come from the Law, and though we depart yet the Law abideth." We see how intensely he believed that salvation depended on works, *i. e.* obedience, and how good works provided a treasury of merit to be shared by others. We see the Jew wrestling with the same problems as St. Paul—Sin, Free-will, and Predestination. Two lines here are very suggestive · " Each one of us hath been the Adam of his own soul " (liv. 19), and " O Adam, what hast thou done to all those who are born of thee ! " They represent in striking phrase the great antinomy which the writer is powerless to resolve Section V. takes us again into the very sphere of St. Paul's thought when he wrote to the Corinthian Christians of the Resurrection Body. With regard to the Messiah there seem to be conflicting views. In xxiv –xxx. the Messianic Kingdom will follow the manifold woes before the judgement; but the Messiah returns to heaven, after being revealed. In the other, *i. e* xxxix , xl., we have a full description of the war of the Messiah against Israel's foes, and of His reign on earth in joy and peace until the Resurrection.

In spite of this the message to the tribes falls back

on a note of utter pessimism, reflecting the evils of
the writer's surroundings:

" For the youth of the world is past
  And the strength of the creation already exhausted,
  And the advent of the times is very short,
  Yea, they have passed by;
  And the pitcher is near to the cistern,
  And the ship to the port,
  And the course of the journey to the city,
  And life to its consummation."   (LXXXV. 10.)

Note.—S P C.K. edition by Charles (1917).

THE GREEK APOCALYPSE OF BARUCH

(III. BARUCH)

THE Greek Apocalypse of Baruch has only recently been translated (1897) by Dr. M. R James from a MS. discovered in the British Museum. It belongs to the early part of the second century, and shows signs, especially in its later part, of having been edited by a Christian writer. It does not bear any close relation to the other Baruch literature, but shows some connection with 1 Enoch. The writer was a Hellenistic Jew, and there is a strong Oriental colour about his speculation. In the latter part the Christian editor, in the vision of the men with baskets, seems to be pointing at the imperfection of the lives and thought of his Jewish opponents.

The Apocalypse relates the journey of Baruch through the five heavens. In the first heaven he sees men " with the faces of oxen, and the horns of stags, and the feet of goats, and the haunches of lambs." These were the builders of the Tower of Babel, and " men like dogs with the feet of stags, the instigators of the building," who took a gimlet, and sought to pierce the heaven, saying, " Let us see whether it is made of clay, or brass, or iron." In the second Baruch sees Hades and the dragon, who eats the bodies of evil-livers, and the tree which led Adam astray. This was the vine planted by Sammael (Satan). In the third he sees the chariot of the sun drawn by forty angels. The Phœnix circles round it, protecting the earth from the sun's rays with the screen of its wings. This wonderful bird lives on manna and dew, and when the angels open the three hundred and sixty-five gates of heaven, it awakens all the cocks on earth with its cry. At evening it stands exhausted with drooping wings, when the angels take away the weary sun's crown to renew it for its next journey; it needs renewal because of the wickedness of men that it has to behold. He also sees the moon, which wanes because of God's anger with her, in that she increased in light when Satan put on the serpent's form, the moon and stars shine by night, when the sun is absent, just as courtiers speak freely only when the king retires. In the fourth the souls of the righteous gather like birds around a pool. In the fifth Michael comes down to the gate of heaven to receive the prayers of man. He holds a deep vessel, in which he carries the merits of the righteous up to God. Men bring their merits in the form of flowers, some of their baskets are full, some half-full, and some empty. Michael rewards the first two classes with oil, and warns the third of coming judgement.

The chief characteristics of the book seem to be its *naive* childishness and accumulation of marvels. Its doctrine of the mediation of the angels, and of the transcendence of God has a gnostic tinge, and is very pronounced. The ethical force of the vision of the men with baskets is stripped of its power, if it is only a piece of religious polemic

As a whole, 3 Baruch takes but a low place among the Apocalypses

Note.—Most accessible in Charles, *Apocrypha and Pseudepigrapha*, Vol. II (Maldwyn Hughes).

THE FOURTH BOOK OF EZRA

THE Fourth Book of Ezra is 2 Esdras of our official Apocrypha. It is therefore better known in the Church than the other apocalyptic writings It is also one of the most interesting, lofty, and deep apocalypses, and presents the spirit of Judaism in a most attractive light. Indeed, it is the writing of one anxiously revolving the enigmas that Christ came to solve, one like St. Paul in outlook, but who has not taken St. Paul's step out of darkness into light.

The book is preserved in Latin, and in Oriental versions. All these are derived from the Greek. And modern scholars may be said to be agreed that this came from a Hebrew original.

Chapters iii–xiv. are the original and important part of the book, the Apocalypse proper Most modern editors since Kabisch (1889) regard these chapters as a composite document, made up of at least five earlier portions : *i e* (i) The First four Visions (Salathiel Apocalypse) ; (ii) The Eagle Vision ; (iii) The Son of Man Vision ; (iv) The Ezra Legend, and (v) Extracts from an old Ezra Apocalypse In any case chapters i. and ii. are a Christian Introduction, and the last two chapters a later piece of Jewish invective. With regard to the date Canon Box places the final editing of chapters iii.–xiv. between A D. 100 and 135 ; the date of the Salathiel portion A.D. 100 ; of the Eagle Vision A D 81–96, or quite possibly A.D. 69–79 ; of the Son of Man Vision before A D. 70 ; the Ezra Legend after A D 70 ; and the old Ezra portion before that date. Its first publication was in the same period as 2 Baruch, to which

it is very similar in some respects.   The Introduction
and Appendix are considerably later.

The book consists of Seven Visions, of which the
following is a brief account:

First Vision, iii. i–v. 13.   In the year 558 B C.
Ezra asks God of the justice of the Captivity and
Fall of Zion.   The angel Uriel sets forth the un-
searchableness of God's ways; only a short time
remains before the end; the signs are described.

Second Vision, v 14–vi 34.   Similar teaching of
man's weak powers, and the coming justification of
God's ways.

Third Vision, vi 35–ix 25   The chief subject is
the fewness of the saved, which moves Ezra's com-
passion intensely   He intercedes for the human race

This section contains a fragment of 69 verses, which
appears in our Revised Version, but not in the Author-
ized Version.   It is missing from most of the Latin
codices, and was recovered by Bensly   It fills the
gap between verses 35 and 36 of the text of the Vulgate, and deals with the Resurrection and Final
Judgement, and the state of the soul in the Inter-
mediate state

Fourth Vision, ix 26–x 59   A woman who has
lost her only son converses with Ezra.   She vanishes,
and in her place he sees a city   He learns that she
represents Zion

Fifth Vision, x 60–xii 39   The Vision of the
Eagle with three heads, and twelve wings, that is
destroyed by a Lion   He is told it is the fourth
kingdom seen by Daniel (*i e.* the Roman power) to
be destroyed by the Messiah.

Sixth Vision, xii. 40–xiii. 58.   The Vision of the
Messiah, who destroys his foes with his word alone,
and then welcomes a peaceful multitude, *i e.* the ten
tribes.

Seventh Vision, xiv. 1–48.   Ezra, warned of his
translation, prays for the people, left without teacher
or Law.   God bids him bring five scribes, and gives
him a wonderful drink, which enables him to dictate

continuously for forty days. The result is ninety-four
books, of which twenty-four are the restored canonical
books that had been destroyed, and seventy are of an
esoteric nature to be preserved by the wise. Ezra's
translation follows.

Whatever view be taken of the original elements
of the book, there is certainly a different tone and
outlook in the earlier and later parts. The earlier
visions are far more deeply concerned with the ulti-
mate problems of human life. The writer is rebellious
and perplexed. Why, he asks, is Israel delivered
over to the heathen? If for punishment, the heathen
surely are equally sinful. And if men by their "evil
heart" are doomed to sin from the beginning, the
Law is only the salvation of a few. The answers to
his despondent questioning are that God is inscrutable,
and man's intelligence limited, that earth's ways have
been fore-ordained, and that in spite of all the love
of God for Israel is "deeper than the measure of
man's mind." He concludes generally in utter
pessimism as to the future of this present order, all
hope lies over the border in the incorruptible world.
Yet even so the problem of the loss of the sinful
remains. Would it not have been better for them
not to have existed? Still he clings to the divine
love, and the hope that "not one life shall be destroyed, or cast as rubbish to the void." In short,
he realizes the failure of the Law, and stands side by
side with St. Paul in his conviction that all have
sinned, and come short of the glory of God, and
therefore that all need mercy.

From this stress on the individual we pass in the
later visions to the more usual ideas of national
restoration. In the Eagle Vision we see a new
theocracy take the place of the Roman tyranny.
In the Son of Man Vision the Messiah rules by the
Law, and his people attain perfection by obedience
to it. In the Ezra Legend the world is very near its
end, and the Messiah will soon appear, and establish
a temporary Messianic Kingdom, which will terminate

in his death, and the return of all things to silence.
Then will follow the Judgement. All this is more or
less parallel with the ideas of the other apocalyptic
writers. It seems to belong to a different world of
thought from that of the writer of the earlier visions
with his obstinate questionings, his sense of the in-
estimable worth of the individual, and his grasp of
the Infinite Pity. If authors were always perfectly
consistent, it would be impossible to regard the earlier
and later visions as the production of one mind.
But it is perhaps allowable to regard him as incon-
sistent and illogical—presenting now the questions
that surged in a deeply sensitive and religious soul,
and now the stereotyped visions of future political
events, which were the common property of the
apocalyptic school. We moderns go to the first
part of his book and hear a brother-mind debating
the same problems that always arise in the human
heart, and leave him refreshed and uplifted, despondent though he be of this world's future, while we
find in the second a picture of what the more commonplace Jewish mind was thinking as to the future of
his race, as he saw the beloved City ruined.

We are indebted to this book for the picturesque story of Ezra rewriting the canonical books,
and for the words of the " Requiem " of Western
Christendom—

" Requiem aeternitatis dabit vobis,
Lux perpetua lucebit vobis."
(II. 34, 35)

Note —Temple Apocrypha edition, by Duff.   S P C K.
edition, by Box (1917).

G

THE PSALMS OF SOLOMON

THE Psalms of Solomon, which only exist now in Greek Manuscripts and one in Syriac, were Hebrew writings, dated by most scholars in the middle of the first century B.C. We find them recognized by the Christian Church up to the sixth century, and returning into notice after long years of oblivion in the seventeenth century.

They are eighteen in number, and, like the canonical Psalms, express the fundamental piety and the deep-set ideals of the Jewish race in hours of stress and crisis. Though not necessarily the work of one author, they are pervaded by a unity of tone and sentiment, which stamps them as the production of one school of thought.

They are distinctly partisan in spirit, and they throw considerable light on the acute antagonism of the Pharisees and Sadducees in the half-century preceding our Lord's birth.

The writers belong to the *Chasidim*, or "godly" Jews, distinctively poor and uninfluential in politics, averse from rebellion against oppression, content to wait for the slow harvest of God's purpose in the coming Messianic Kingdom, rigorous in their fulfilment of the commands of the Law, passionately pure in sexual matters, firm believers in a future life, and holding the balance even between fate and freewill in the manner of the later Pharisees described by Josephus.

The Psalms denounce those opposed to all such ideals, whom we shall be right in identifying with the Sadducees. From the point of view of the writers the latter are characteristically "sinful," loose in morals, and careless of the honour of the Sanctuary, with which they had a very close connection. They possessed wealth and political influence, which was based upon their support of the later Hasmonæan king-priests By their sins they had drawn down upon their country the storm of Roman invasion, merging good and bad alike in common ruin, and the prophetic insight of the Psalmist foresees for them no portion in the world to come but utter destruction.

Thus in these Psalms we have a very striking picture of the intense bitterness of feeling between the two chief religious parties of that day, a bitterness which saw no trace of good in its opponents, and exaggerated their feelings with relentless severity.

The references to the "alien conqueror" seem to fix the date of these writings unmistakably, as well as to show the attitude of Jewish Quietists to the Romans. Though these have been referred to Antiochus Epiphanes, there can be little question that they point far more directly to Pompey the Great, and his capture of Jerusalem in 48 B C. They tell of one who came from the West, and was allowed by those in power to approach Jerusalem without opposition, who, when at last he found himself opposed, stormed Mount Zion with battering-rams, defiled the altar, carried captives away with him, and eventually perished amid the sands of Egypt, where he lay on the shore without burial. Now all this is remarkably close to what actually happened in the case of Pompey, and we are justified in regarding the Psalms as the product of a time when these tragedies were not long past.

Continuing the prophetic attitude to foreign invaders like Cyrus, Pompey is seen by the writer as an Avenger sent by God Himself—

> " He captured the fortresses and the wall of
>   Jerusalem ;
> For God Himself led him in safety, while
>   they wandered."   (VIII 21)

It was a necessary doom, a flood that swept away defilement, and left " the servants of God like innocent lambs in the midst," to adore the righteousness and faithfulness of God. It was the proper harvest of the days when " the king was a transgressor, and the judge disobedient, and the people sinful." And now it is past, the Advent of the true King, the Son of David, may be looked for. Nowhere in these writings is the picture of the Messiah more beautifully drawn than in Psalm xvii. He is the Righteous Deliverer freeing Israel by " the word of his mouth," and driving unrighteousness away. He is the Universalist Messiah " who shall have the heathen nations to serve under his yoke." He is the model king " who himself shall be pure from sin, that he may rule a great people."

As a short example of the general spirit of these Psalms, I will select the sixth—

VI. IN HOPE: OF SOLOMON

Happy is the man, whose heart is fixed to call upon the name of the Lord;

When he remembereth the name of the Lord he will be saved.

His ways are made even by the Lord,

And the works of his hands are preserved by the Lord his God.

At what he seeth in his bad dreams his soul shall not be troubled;

When he passeth through rivers, and the tossing of seas, he shall not be dismayed;

He ariseth from sleep and blesseth the name of the Lord;

When his heart is at peace he singeth to the name of his God:

And he entreateth the Lord for all his house.

And the Lord heareth the prayer of every one that feareth God,

And every request of the soul that hopeth for Him
   doth the Lord accomplish.
Blessed is the Lord, who sheweth mercy to those who
   love Him in sincerity.

Note —Editions by Ryle and James (1891) and Rendel
Harris (1911), and S.P C K. edition, by Box.

THE FOURTH BOOK OF MACCABEES

THE book known to us as the Fourth Book of
Maccabees appears among the works of Josephus
under the title " On the Supremacy of Reason " ;
but it is almost impossible to regard it as written
by him.

Internal evidence seems to show that it was written
between 60 B.C. and A.D. 38, the date of the persecution
of the Emperor Caligula.

Its author must have been a learned and cultured
Jewish rhetorician, teaching most probably in Alexandria, the meeting-place of Hebrew and Hellenic
thought. He is quite at home with the phraseology
of Greek philosophy, and writes as a Stoic, but at the
same time holds his orthodox faith firmly, and teaches
that the ideals of Stoic virtue are best reached by
those who are trained under the Law of Moses. He
thus blends for us the culture of the Greek and of the
Jew in a way that must have been common in our
Lord's time.

The book is either a sermon for the synagogue, or
a rhetorical exercise of the nature of a lecture, very
much worked-up and somewhat florid in its manner.
Its object seems to be to stiffen the spirits of Jewish
hearers by recalling the heroism of the martyrs of
their race in the days of Antiochus Epiphanes, more
than a century before.

The thesis of the discourse is that the Reason of
man exists to control his passions, and to assure the
balance of character by the attainment of the right
measure of the four Stoic virtues of judgement, justice,
courage, and temperance. Unlike the Stoic, however,
the writer teaches that the passions are grounded in

human nature, and only need control, not destruction. He is saner and more human than the Stoic. As illustrations of his thesis he refers to the lives of Joseph, Jacob, Moses, and David, and then describes at length the heroic martyrdom of Eleazar, and the Seven Brethren and their mother, by Antiochus. He gives us the tragic conversations between the tyrant and his victims—the old man Eleazar, the seven brothers and their noble mother, who are all examples of the power of Reason to make men true to their principles in spite of the severest strain of suffering. In a flood of eulogy he claims that such martyrs not only attain a heavenly reward, but save their country by disarming and shaming the tyrant. In the last chapter the writer imagines the mother implanting the spirit in which they died, by recalling their dead father's teaching from the Law and the prophets about the great heroes of their race.

The description of the tortures is often gruesome in the extreme. We have " wheels, joint-dislocators, and racks, and bone-crushers, and catapults, and chaldrons, and braziers, and thumb-screws, and iron claws, and wedges, and branding-irons," employed by the tyrant to break down the constancy of the youths, until the last and youngest being allowed to go free to speak to him and those round him, proudly denounces him and leaps into a red-hot brazier. The persuasions of the tyrant are made most alluring, the torment unspeakably horrible, yet they remained firm, and their mother pressed them on. So the conclusion is—

" How can we do otherwise than admit right Reason's mastery over passion with those men who shrank not before the agonies of burning? For even as towers on harbour-moles repulse the assaults of the waves, and offer a calm entrance to those entering the haven, so the seven-towered right Reason of the youths defended the haven of righteousness, and repulsed the tempestuousness of the passions. They formed a holy choir of righteousness, as they cheered one another on, saying, ' Let us die like brothers, O brethren, for the Law. Let us imitate the Three Children at the Assyrian court, who despised this same ordeal, the furnace.' . . . Let us then own ourselves with divine Reason's mastery of the passions. After this our passion Abraham, Isaac and Jacob shall receive us, and all our forefathers shall praise us.''

The writer exhausts himself in the eulogy of the mother. She overcame the primitive instincts which work just as much in the animal world as in human nature ; for a mother's love "becomes the centre of her whole world.'' She overcame by Reason " nature and parenthood and mother-love and her children on the rack,'' and became like the Ark of Noah, a bearer of the burden of the future. For by her fidelity she upheld for coming generations the burden of the Law of God.

The Fourth Book of Maccabees is interesting as being the ground of a free paraphrase, in another era of persecution, by the great Erasmus. It certainly is a vivid picture of the spirit of the martyrs of all ages, and it is no wonder that it has spoken with something of a clarion-voice to the Church in times when fidelity to the Truth meant peril of death.

Note.—S P C.K edition, by Emmet (1918).

THE BIBLICAL ANTIQUITIES OF PHILO

IN the so-called Biblical Antiquities of Philo we have an instance of the rediscovery for the use of students of our own day of a piece of Jewish literature, most probably of the same date as a great part of the New Testament. Dr. M. R. James, its translator and editor, found some fragments of this work in 1893 in a manuscript at Cheltenham, which led to their being identified with part of a Jewish work, which had been sufficiently well-known during the Revival of Learning in the sixteenth century to be printed in at least five editions. Its history through the Middle Ages is very obscure, and there are no certain allusions to it in the Fathers, unless it be in Origen [On John (Tom. vi. 14)]. Modern scholars regard it as a valuable addition to our sources of knowledge of the orthodox Jewish mind after the Fall of Jerusalem A.D. 70, and as closely connected with the school of writers who produced the Fourth Book of Esdras and the Apocalypse of Baruch. Its attribution to Philo is a vagary of which there is no explanation, and the title was probably appended in the sixteenth century.

There seems no doubt that, like the Assumption of Moses, it was originally written in Hebrew, then translated into Greek, and that our somewhat corrupt and imperfect Latin Version was made in the fourth century.

All that remains of the book includes a more or less continuous history of Israel from Adam to the death of Saul. It is suggested that the Books of Chronicles were its model, but in reading it we are

not conscious of anything of the nature of the pre-
dominating priestly tendency of the chroniclers. The
writer's purpose in neglecting or scantily epitomizing
wide fields of Biblical material, in rewriting lives and
speeches, and in concentrating attention on persons
and events hardly known in the Bible can only be
guessed at. His long lists of names and imaginary
numbers are a strange evidence of what pleased the
Jews of that time. Dr. James supposes that he desired to fill out the existing narratives and " to infuse
a more religious tone into certain episodes of the
history, particularly into the period of the Judges,
and to emphasize certain great truths, foremost
among which should be placed the indestructibility
of Israel, and the duty of faithfulness to the One
God."

This book is thus similar in scope to the Book of
Jubilees; it is an attempt to rewrite the early part
of the Old Testament. But (i) Jubilees is chiefly
concerned with the Patriarchs, whereas " Philo"
gives most space to the Judges and Saul. (ii) Jubilees is definitely anxious to exalt the ceremonial
Law and the Temple system, while " Philo" shows
no sense of this side of Pharisaism. (iii) Jubilees
works up ancient legends and comments, whereas
" Philo" seems to be largely using his own imagination, in the creation, for instance, of the heroic Kenaz,
whom one can hardly suppose the readers were
intended to regard as a historical personage.

With regard to the writer the general impression
of him is admirably summarized by Dr. James [1]:

" We cannot regard him as a man of very lofty
mind or of great literary talent. He has some
imagination, and is sensible of the majesty of the Old
Testament literature, but he has not the insight, the
power, or the earnestness of the author of 4 Esdras,
nor again the ethical perception of him who wrote
the Testaments of the Twelve Patriarchs."

[1] p 65.

The writer has several expressions similar to those in the New Testament, showing the use of a common language among religious writers. St. Paul's Rock[1] that followed the Israelites in the wilderness is usefully illustrated (x. 7) : "He brought them quails from the sea, and a well of water following them brought he forth for them." And xi. 15 : "And there did he command many things and showed him the tree of life, whereof he cut and took and put it into Mara, and the Water of Mara was made sweet and followed them in the desert forty years, and went up into the hills with them, and came down into the plain." In cxlviii. we find an interesting identification of Phinehas with Elijah, illustrating the hint in St. Mark ix. 13 ("As it is written of him") that the Jewish tradition was that Elijah, when he came again, should suffer death.

The book teaches that there will be a judgement according to works at the end of the world, and a new heaven and a new earth, in which the righteous shall dwell with Moses, lighted by the precious stones of their ancient temple, and mutually recognizing one another. The wicked will pine in hell till the end of the world and will then be destroyed. The stress on retribution is very marked ; sooner or later the punishment for sin comes. The idea of Israel's privilege is very majestic : Israel alone exists to glorify God, she can never be utterly destroyed, her Law is the everlasting canon by which the world will be judged. Her chief danger is to mingle in marriage with the Gentiles. With regard to the spirit-world, there is an allusion to guardian-angels, to angels as intercessors for men, and to angels, whose names are given (Ingethal, Zeruch, Nathaniel), set over the hidden things, strength, and fire. Evil spirits are not very prominent, but we have the touch in Samuel's Vision, that Eli wonders if an unclean spirit has spoken ; for if one hears two calls at night the speaker is an evil spirit, if three, God. The conception of God is very

[1] 1 Cor. xi. 4, and Targum of Onkelos on Numbers

interesting, as showing what popular ideas Christianity actually displaced. He is certainly " All Light " to Moses, and " Life," and " One who looks on the heart," and He knows the minds of all generations before they are born—but He punishes Jephtha by the loss of his daughter, because his vow angered Him : " If a dog were the first to meet him, should a dog be offered to Me ? It shall fall upon his only child." He is deceitful and spiteful; *e.g.* he will not allow Eli's sons to repent, " because aforetime they had said : When we grow old we will repent."

Dr. James does not find any anticipation of a Messiah in the text. God works and will complete His work, according to the writer, without an intermediary.

The sixty-five chapters of the book are filled as follows—

I.–II. Adam to Lamech.

III.–V. Noah and his descendants.

VI.–VIII. Abraham to the death of Joseph.

IX.–XIX. Moses.

XX –XXIV. Joshua.

XXV –XLIII. The Judges.

XLIV.–XLVIII. Events of the last chapters of Judges

XLIX –LV. Life of Samuel to the return of the Ark

LVI.–LVIII. Saul's career.

LIX.–LXV. Saul and David to Saul's death.

The large amount of space devoted to the Judges is striking, and the fact that a third of it has to do with " Kenaz " still more so. He immediately succeeds Joshua, emulates him in discovering hidden sinners, and in martial deeds. The account of his combat with the Amorites is interesting, but scarcely a fair example of the writer's style :

XXVII. 10 : "And it came to pass when Cerez heard their words he was clothed with the spirit of might and changed into another man, and went down into the camp of the Amorites and began to smite them. And the Lord sent before his face the angel Ingethal, who is set over the hidden things, and worketh unseen, (and another) angel of might helping with him; and Ingethal smote the Amorites with blindness, so that every man that saw his neighbour counted them his adversaries, and they slew one another. And the angel Zeruch, who is set over strength, bare up the arms of Cerez lest they should perceive him; and Cerez smote of the Amorites forty and five thousand men, and they themselves smote one another; And fell forty and five thousand men. 11. And when Cerez had smitten a great multitude, he would have loosened his hand from his sword, for the handle of the sword clave, that it could not be loosed, and his right hand had taken into it the strength of the sword."

Note.—S P C.K. edition, by James (1917).

INDEX

www.ingramcontent.com/pod-product-compliance
Lightning Source LLC
Chambersburg PA
CBHW071946100426

42736CB00042B/2214